FRONT-E
DEVELO

BCS, THE CHARTERED INSTITUTE FOR IT

BCS, The Chartered Institute for IT, is committed to making IT good for society. We use the power of our network to bring about positive, tangible change. We champion the global IT profession and the interests of individuals, engaged in that profession, for the benefit of all.

Exchanging IT expertise and knowledge
The Institute fosters links between experts from industry, academia and business to promote new thinking, education and knowledge sharing.

Supporting practitioners
Through continuing professional development and a series of respected IT qualifications, the Institute seeks to promote professional practice tuned to the demands of business. It provides practical support and information services to its members and volunteer communities around the world.

Setting standards and frameworks
The Institute collaborates with government, industry and relevant bodies to establish good working practices, codes of conduct, skills frameworks and common standards. It also offers a range of consultancy services to employers to help them adopt best practice.

Become a member
Over 70,000 people including students, teachers, professionals and practitioners enjoy the benefits of BCS membership. These include access to an international community, invitations to a roster of local and national events, career development tools and a quarterly thought-leadership magazine. Visit www.bcs.org/membership to find out more.

Further information
BCS, The Chartered Institute for IT,
First Floor, Block D,
North Star House, North Star Avenue,
Swindon, SN2 1FA, United Kingdom.
T +44 (0) 1793 417 417
(Monday to Friday, 09:00 to 17:00 UK time)
www.bcs.org/contact
http://shop.bcs.org/

FRONT-END DEVELOPER

Dominic Myers

Published by BCS Learning & Development Ltd, a wholly owned subsidiary of BCS, The Chartered Institute for IT, First Floor, Block D, North Star House, North Star Avenue, Swindon, SN2 1FA, UK.
www.bcs.org

Paperback ISBN: 978-1-78017-4761
PDF ISBN: 978-1-78017-4778
ePUB ISBN: 978-1-78017-4785
Kindle ISBN: 978-1-78017-4792

British Cataloguing in Publication Data.
A CIP catalogue record for this book is available at the British Library.

Publisher's acknowledgements
Reviewers: Chris Benge, Pieter van der Westhuizen and Mark Berthelemy
Publisher: Ian Borthwick
Commissioning editor: Becky Youé
Production manager: Florence Leroy
Project manager: Hazel Bird
Copy-editor: Hazel Bird
Proofreader: Barbara Eastman
Indexer: Sally Roots
Cover design: Alex Wright
Cover image: AgriTech
Typeset by Lapiz Digital Services, Chennai, India
Printed by Hobbs the Printers Ltd

CONTENTS

LIST OF FIGURES AND TABLE

AUTHOR

Dominic Myers is a front-end developer with a wealth of professional experience. He spends most of his day being fascinated by, developing and implementing the newest trends in web development, and primarily works in HTML, CSS and JavaScript – though he is happy to use whatever will get the job done. Before switching to software development, he was a psychiatric nurse for longer than he cares to remember. He shares his knowledge online via his blog (https://drmsite. blogspot.com) as well as contributing to forums such as Stack Overflow.

ACKNOWLEDGEMENTS

I want to thank my wife, Katrina Myers, for putting up with me while I was writing this book. My whole family have been immensely supportive while I've been absent at weekends (thanks Mum, Dad, Oz and Ash). Notable professional mentions include Lars Malmqvist, Denis Kaminskiy and Alex Weinle at Arcus Global Ltd and the whole team at Vigilant Software, but I would like to thank all those who have helped me in my second career – you know who you are (Witchford Archers rock!). And, of course, Becky and Hazel have done a magnificent job of wrestling my awkward prose into shape.

PREFACE

This book serves as an introduction to the role of a front-end[1] developer, sometimes known by other titles, such as web developer or user interface (UI) developer. Primarily this will be within the realm of web-based applications, but increasingly front-end developers will have their work viewed on mobile devices too; this means that the traditional website now not only is seen on a monitor but also has to cater for very many other screen sizes and aspect ratios. Many of the skills employed by front-end developers are of relevance to applications developed for mobile platforms, and the skills you learn as a front-end developer will allow you to develop apps for platforms such as Android and iOS.

Front-end developers are everywhere, but you shouldn't notice the good ones – unless, that is, you are delighted by something truly exceptional in your interaction with a system. All front-end developers aim to produce that delight but know that it is fleeting; for instance, who now remembers the creator of the infamous hamburger? (It was Norm Cox (Vo, 2015).) Joy is gratifying but momentary; what was once delightful will become commonplace, so the bar to producing delight is forever rising. We also know that if you do not notice our work, then we have done it well. If you use a system without having to overthink, keeping your concentration on the task at hand rather than the tools you are using, then we will have succeeded.

---

[1] The front-end is anything which we display to our users via markup. The rest of this book will go into far greater detail about this and about why there is a distinction between the front-end and back-end of an application. Note that this book tends to use the words 'application' and 'website' interchangeably.

In this book, we will explore the role of the front-end developer and our purpose, responsibilities and skills.

Along with the things a front-end developer should be aware of, we will discuss some of the tools you will need to become familiar with, if you are not already. We will also look at some less concrete attributes of the role, such as empathy and compassion, and explore ways of cultivating them within ourselves.

Finally, we will explore the working life of a front-end developer and expand upon those things that might be of relevance to you in your career.

This book contains the code for various layout techniques. The code can also be accessed here: https://jsfiddle.net/ annoyingmouse/896v2jhL. In this book, the formatting of the code has sometimes been altered to improve the layout on the page.

1 THE FRONT-END DEVELOPER

In this chapter, we discuss what we mean by the term 'front-end' as well as the need for a dedicated front-end developer within modern development teams.

WHAT IS A FRONT-END DEVELOPER?

Historically, computers were people: a room full of mathematicians tasked with carrying out calculations. Humans are fallible, though, so there were many early attempts to automate the process of computation, such as the Babbage Engine (Computer History Museum, n.d.). Computers, as we know them, are a much more recent development.

When the more modern computers initially came about, they were less than user friendly, and users were left trying to fit their heads into the computer space – trying to fit complex thoughts and concepts into ones and zeros. Users of those early electronic computers were sometimes seen as strange and aloof, having to spend their time thinking in a way that a computer would understand, altering the registers of a processor using assembly languages.[1] Often these users were also the programmers or developers of the computer and could be seen as having a symbiotic relationship with the hardware. If they needed the computer to do something, they

---

1   While not the lowest level of programming language, assembly languages are about the lowest level which can be understood by people who do not design chips used in the solving of calculations. Different processor architectures have different assembly languages, but they all have similar sets of instructions.

needed to be able to tell the computer to do that thing in a way that the machine could understand.

Even those early computers were massively powerful compared to a room full of mathematicians, and far less likely to make mistakes, but they were costly and required a massive infrastructure. Business, governments and universities required some return on the enormous investment the computers represented, so the original users were asked to program the computers to undertake specific tasks, thus becoming specialist developers. The developer then came to be something of an interface between the user and the computer.

Alan Skorkin has written about the distinctions between developers, programmers and computer scientists (Skorkin, 2010). He says that, while he uses the terms interchangeably (as many do), people he meets in the industry often classify themselves as falling into a single category.

There was often a further requirement for someone to act as an interpreter between the user and the developer, and so the roles of the systems analyst and designer were born, introducing yet another layer.

While systems analysts are aware of the needs of the actual users of a system, they are also responsible for its overall design. As such, the idea of them having specialist knowledge of how a user interacts with a system might seem excessive; thus, the specialist role of the front-end developer came into play.

The front-end developer is the member of the team whose work has the closest impact on the user, despite often never encountering them. Whereas the back-end developer is concerned with the logic of the application and will use a plethora of tools to ensure that that logic is maintained during interactions with the user, the front-end developer uses a significantly different toolset to ensure that the logic is presented in a way that makes sense to users and is aesthetically pleasing.

I find it useful, as a front-end developer, to imagine my parents interacting with a system I am developing. My mum is not one of those parents who can send an SMS, and all her interactions are in person or by voice over the phone. She is getting better at interacting online and with banks, and she now shops on the internet, but there was a time when I worried that she would be unable to communicate with larger and larger portions of the modern discourse.

Conversely, my dad is sometimes overly cautious and less nuanced than some users, being quick to end an online interaction at the least provocation, fearing that someone might steal his personal information and do goodness knows what with it. I am sure we all know someone who feels left out of some aspects of the modern world because they are not comfortable using a computer, but should they have to lose out or should we do all in our power to make their interactions as painless as possible?

What do we mean when we use the term 'front-end development'? Wikipedia has a good definition: 'the practice of converting data to graphical interface for user[s] to view and interact with data through digital interaction using HTML [Hypertext Markup Language], CSS [Cascading Style Sheets] and JavaScript' (Wikipedia, 2018). The front-end is anything which we display to our users via markup.

3

I once went to a party in London not long after starting work as a front-end developer. When I was asked what I did for a living, I said that I made the stuff which Lars Malmqvist (my boss at the time) did 'look pretty'. I expanded, as at the time we were primarily involved in allowing residents of the Royal Borough of Windsor and Maidenhead to interrogate a data set, by noting that Lars did the hard stuff by extracting, manipulating and subsequently geofencing the data, while I was merely responsible for displaying it on a map.

At the time, we had either just been shortlisted for or won the 2011 Guardian's Megas award (The Guardian, 2011), and both we and our primary investor were rightly pleased as punch.

Saying that front-end developers merely make things look pretty is perhaps disingenuous, though. Ivan Codesido explained, when he wrote in *The Guardian* in 2009, that the front-end developer (or 'client-side developer', as he calls the job) aims to:

> Create clear, easy, fast pages and interfaces that will make people understand and care about the information, by putting it in context, expose its legitimacy or lack thereof, and reveal [the information's] implicit or explicit interconnection. (Codesido, 2009)

While Codesido seems to have a bias towards a journalistic interpretation of what a front-end developer is, this is probably not such a wrong approach to take to the role. We might be tasked with creating content (see the section in Chapter 3 on images) but, generally, we are the people tasked with creating a meaningful experience for users from artefacts generated by others, be those images or text.

I would also expand upon Codesido's definition by noting that we need to allow our users to interact with the services which we present in as simple a way as possible. For example, our users might not be working afront a multi-monitor display with access to a fast broadband connection but might be struggling to interact with a form via a feature phone over a slow mobile connection. Using empathy to imagine such scenarios will help us to appreciate making the experiences we are crafting as efficient as possible, for as many users as possible. Squeezing as much extraneous data as possible from an image, while keeping it clear, might seem a waste of effort as it downloads to our machines in a minuscule fraction of a second while we are at work; for some of our users, though, the delayed image download, over slower connections, might mean that they miss some vital information or lose patience. This may either lose clients an interaction or users an opportunity.

The distinction between clients and users is the mainstay of the role of the front-end developer, and we offer something of an intersection between the two spheres. Ideally, no one should have two masters, but in this instance we should be conscious of our responsibilities to both, being unafraid to challenge either while being mindful of their distinct needs. When the needs of both masters are in concordance, we should also aim to gently challenge them, even if just by presenting new elements to them to keep their interest piqued.

Also in 2009, Paul Carvill, a colleague of Codesido, wrote about the history of front-end developers and noted that the role only really started to mature in the last few years of the previous millennium (Carvill, 2009). He suggests that much of this was down to Google's search algorithm and an appreciation that data could best be discovered, and thus indexed, when presented semantically. I will expand upon semantics later, but in this instance we are talking about the structure of the underlying data.

We can present data in all sorts of ways as front-end developers (as evidenced on the CSS Zen Garden site (Shea, 2005)), but not all of these methods are suited to the information being parsed by search engines. How much better to target our efforts at search engines as well as our users and reduce effort, allowing both our users and other (perhaps intelligent) agents to glean what is pertinent?

Carvill goes on to note that front-end developers require a vast skill set (with a similarly massive job description). I will discuss the main tools of our trade in the next chapter. While their scope can seem daunting, the challenges offered are more than rewarded both in terms of personal satisfaction and monetarily.

The Hawaii missile alert in 2018 – when an alarm was broadcast to the population of Hawaii saying that there was an incoming ballistic missile and that the community should seek shelter – is an example of how weak front-end development can have disastrous results. Core77 (Noe, 2016) shows the original screen where the error was made. It seems to have been a matter of someone clicking on the wrong hyperlink in a document containing two very similar instructions: one with the word 'DRILL' at the start.

While there were no reports of fatalities occurring as a result of the Hawaii missile alert, ill-thought-out design has been linked with deaths (Shariat, 2014). You must be aware of your responsibilities. It may well be that you will not be developing such vital infrastructures as missile alert systems or medical interfaces, but you have a responsibility to communicate either your or your employer's vision in as clear a way as possible. Users' lives might not depend upon it, but they will take away something from every interaction, if only subconsciously.

FRONT-END DEVELOPER RESPONSIBILITIES

When you see job specifications for front-end developer roles, there will be countless responsibilities listed, but they all encompass the following items.

Design, creation and maintenance of websites

The design, creation and maintenance of websites make up a considerable portion of the front-end developer's responsibilities, and we will look at critical aspects of these tasks later in this book. There are many tools available to aid you with the design of websites, including merely a pen and paper. You might even be in the fortunate position of having a designer who will furnish you with a design. Wherever the design comes from, you then have to implement it using Hypertext Markup Language (HTML), Cascading Style Sheets (CSS) and JavaScript – we will examine each of these in the next chapter.

Keeping abreast of technology

As you will see in the following chapters, the environment of the front-end developer is continually changing, with standards being adapted and new technologies, approaches, fashions and techniques appearing all the time, while others are either superseded or removed altogether. Being aware of current trends and techniques is of paramount importance and helps with the maintenance clause of the first responsibility, as it will help you not only to improve your future work but also to enhance your previous work.

Communication

I mentioned earlier that all developers need to be aware of the requirements of two, sometimes converging, groups (clients and eventual users). Alongside being able to communicate effectively with clients and users, we sometimes find ourselves working within a larger team and so being able to communicate with colleagues is of importance. We will look at the elements of effective communication at greater length later in this book, but please note that you may well have to communicate with your future self. Having clean and well-documented code not only is professional but will also help you and your colleagues in the future.

Testing and validating

Traditional testing in the front-end can be fraught with issues with regard to waiting for asynchronous JavaScript and XML (AJAX) calls to complete before checking the resulting markup; alongside those issues, we might also test our work with all or a subset of users or others. Whatever the nature of the testing you embark upon, having a plan is the pre-eminent concern. There is a wealth of tools available to help with traditional testing of the front-end, and we will go into greater depth regarding researching and testing your work with your users in Chapter 3. Validation of markup can be bundled into the first point, as it will be your duty to produce valid markup – while appreciating that not all browsers treat markup identically; services such as the World Wide Web Consortium (W3C) Markup Validation Service will prove invaluable.

THE CONTEXT OF THE FRONT-END DEVELOPER

This book is about the front-end developer, but working purely within a front-end developer silo is not something that I would encourage. Maintaining a silo mentality, and not understanding the roles of those you are working with, means that you are unable to make their lives easier. Being helpful will encourage reciprocation, and they will be more inclined to make your life more comfortable in return; casting your eye over their pull requests,[2] for example, will help you to understand the overall application you are working on, and you might be able to spot glaring syntax errors.

---

2   A pull request is a way that a member of a team can ask to make changes to the code in a Git repository.

Full-stack developers

A full-stack developer is a developer who codes both the back-end and the front-end of an application. They might not have the specialist knowledge required to be classed as a specialist front-end or a specialist back-end developer, but this can vary: some have a leaning towards one rather than the other, and others may be experts in both.

Full-stack developers are highly sought after, no matter the technology stack they favour, due to their versatility.

There are arguments about the validity of the term 'full-stack developer', with some claiming it to be a trend and nothing more, as most developers have some knowledge of other aspects of the stack. Indeed, some suggest that to be defined as a full-stack developer, a developer needs to have knowledge and appreciation of all levels of the 'stack', from the underlying networked structure of HTTP (Hypertext Transfer Protocol) requests all the way up to the needs of the business (Yellvula, 2017).

That is not to suggest that employing a full-stack developer negates the need for a dedicated front-end developer, as they often work well together – a full-stack developer might create the overall application, while the front-end developer might then provide suitable polish and check that the finished product works well for the user.

Back-end developers

What we do, as front-end developers, is to provide a veneer to what back-end developers make and, for want of a better phrase, make it look appealing. Most interactions with a web application will entail some server-side code taking what we send and processing it in some way. Back-end developers are not limited to this processing, though; they need to understand the database they will be using for the storage of that data and the peculiarities of the operating system upon which both the server and the database reside. They also need to collaborate with business stakeholders to understand the needs that their code will address. There is a huge choice of programming languages that back-end developers can use.

> Once you have a familiarity with one programming language, you will find that you can parse others and subsequently gain some understanding of what is going on.

A good working relationship with a back-end developer is paramount. The back-end developer is responsible for the hidden parts of the application, the code that connects to the database and handles any CRUD (create, read, update and delete) operations on it while ensuring the consistency of any data saved, as well as its conformance with business logic. The role is undoubtedly essential, but without the user being able to interact with this code, there is no application – this is where the experience of the front-end developer comes into play. Simple HTML inputs suffice for most operations but ensuring that interacting with the application is not onerous is our responsibility; our aim should be to develop pleasing and unique ways for our users to interact with the underlying code. If we don't understand what the back-end developer requires from us, we can be left floundering.

> Some of my most satisfying development experiences have been working alongside a software architect working as a back-end developer – Andy Widdess. We got loads done in quite a short period of time, with him asking me what I wanted in terms of data from the back-end and, in turn, telling me what he expected to receive.

10

Working in such a way was extraordinarily satisfying and productive. It was one of those partnerships which are rare, and, although it did not last long enough, while we were performing so synergistically we managed to get a great deal of the application written.

During our project, we had some discussion about how much he should manipulate the data returned in his APIs (application programming interfaces) and how much I should, when returning data to the server. This mixing of concerns is like that of CSS and JavaScript becoming closer in their abilities to change the user interface (UI). I was more than capable of producing data in a form suited to the back-end while being able to process the data received so that it was better suited to the UI. My colleague made my life easier by doing the heavy lifting on the server – we came to an amicable resolution which allowed us both the opportunity to wrangle the data enough to satisfy us.

Software architect

Like the software designer, discussed below, the software architect is responsible for the choices made in development but at a higher level. For example, they might be responsible for defining and enforcing standards such as coding practices, ensuring comments are in place.

The software architect designs the overarching structure of an application, the software designer ensures that the bits hang together, and the other developers build the application. Sometimes the software architect and software designer can be involved with the development as well; however, this is less likely in larger teams, as they spend significant amounts of time managing those responsible for the actual code.

Depending on the level of detail of the architect's design of the finished plan, having a relationship with them will allow them

11

to better judge what is possible as well as desirable within the application. Giving them the benefit of your understanding of the needs of your users will allow them to better architect the application so that it makes sense to the user. To an extent, you need to be an advocate for the user.

Software designer

Whereas a software architect develops the overall skeleton of the application, the software designer is responsible for fleshing out the skeleton. As such they are often more experienced developers, as this allows them to guide other developers and make decisions about the specific implementation of the designs of the software architect.

The team's software designer often attends architecture meetings, where the wider application and the roadmap of future developments are discussed, and subsequently uses regular review meetings to filter these down to the rest of the team. Having a good relationship with them is essential so that you feel able to bring suggestions to the table when discussing their proposed implementation of the architecture. If you can suggest novel and visually pleasing approaches to designing an interaction, then they can consider these when it comes to their design.

Scrum master

Scrum is a methodology which allows a team to self-organise, though there needs to be a specific facilitator. This role is called the Scrum master, and this can be a dedicated person (either for a single team or for multiple teams), or it can rotate among different members of the team. Perhaps the best description of the role comes from a video available on YouTube (GroetenUitDelft, 2011) and sponsored by Scrum.nl (Prowareness, 2018). This light-hearted depiction of the position touches on the main points of the role, and it sort of mirrors the actions of an effective chair within a meeting, in that the chair encourages the flow of information in the daily stand-up,[3] not only helping every member of the team to speak and describe what they have done and what they plan to do now, but also gently reigning in a boisterous team if necessary.

This lightness of touch is also critical when it comes to addressing team dynamics. Behaviour such as bullying needs to be addressed, and the Scrum master often takes the role of an impartial adjudicator; team dynamics are at least as important as anything else. You may have the most skilled front-end and back-end developers, but if they do not get on and are incapable of talking to each other, then the project and business will suffer. As mentioned earlier, being able to communicate well is likely to be one of your most essential skills as a front-end developer – the Scrum master is there to encourage this, especially for those of your colleagues who might find it uncomfortable.

As well as encouraging appropriate communication within the team, a Scrum master acts as a filter or mediator between the team and others. They also help to overcome any barriers or blockers confronting the team. Sometimes this can be as simple as ensuring there is the proper equipment, software licences or permissions in place.

Should Scrum master be a role you are interested in, I will share advice from transformation coach Melvyn Pullen, who suggests reading the official Scrum guide (Sutherland & Schwaber, 2018) over and over again.

Having a dedicated Scrum master might be the best way of organising a team as they will have some experience of Agile[4] and Scrum and might even hold a relevant qualification. They

3   A stand-up is where members of the development team can inform each other of their progress, what their development plans are for the day and any impediments to that progress they might be facing.
4   Making applications can be very complicated. The Agile methodology can help to ease this complexity by breaking the work into small, manageable chunks.

might be affiliated with any number of bodies such as Scrum.org or the Scrum Alliance (2018).

Smaller or younger teams might get by using a rotating Scrum master; alternatively, a member of the team might be assigned the role full time, with a corresponding reduction in other duties to allow them time to fulfil the responsibilities of their new position.

I have heard reports of workplaces where team members were appointed as Scrum masters full time. However, it seems that those with these extra duties often did not find that their original workload reduced – and, in those places where it did, they often felt frustrated that their supplemental work got in the way of the things that they found most fulfilling.

Product owner

Whereas the Scrum master might be equated with a sergeant in the armed forces, the product owner has a more strategic view and could be likened to a commissioned officer. They have the responsibility for managing the backlog of work with which the whole team will eventually be tasked. The backlog represents something of a roadmap or plan for what will be delivered, and to an extent it is never-ending.[5]

As it can be represented as a pool of tasks, the backlog needs to be organised so that related features, bug fixes, stories[6] and non-functional requirements[7] are delivered logically. It would make no sense for the front-end architecture to be in place before the back-end were produced, or vice versa, as there

---

5   'Backlog' is an Agile term (see Chapter 3 for more on Agile).
6   'Stories' is an Agile term (see Chapter 3 for more on Agile). It is a high-level definition of a requirement which allows developers to estimate the effort required to implement it.
7   A functional requirement specifies what the system should do, whereas non-functional requirements describe how the system should work.

would be a delay in the finished aspect of the application being released, as it is a combination of the two ends of development.

Note that there can often be a disconnect in the process of bringing the front-end and the back-end together. I believe that the best solution is for both to be developed in concert, but this can be difficult to orchestrate in practice. I have found it useful to work up a prototype structure for the back-end using some dummy data, which later allows the full-stack developer to take my data structure and put flesh on its bones with the actual data from the database.

The person tasked with the organisation of the backlog is the product owner, and they must balance the needs of the business with the needs and abilities of the development team. While the Scrum master should mediate communication between the team and the product owner, it is sometimes useful to gain clarification directly from the product owner, especially if they work closely with the designer. Being a front-end developer means that aesthetics is going to be at the forefront of your work, and gaining clarification directly from the person likely to sign off your work, rather than deal with further changes later, will save time. That is not to suggest that clarification from the product owner is only required by front-end developers – all team members might need such explanation, so some negotiation must be sought from the Scrum master to understand whether it is acceptable to them to be bypassed in such a way.

It is sometimes the case that the product owner is known as the 'single wringable neck' (Hartman, 2009) as they are the person with the overall responsibility for the work and the order in which it is carried out. They are in a position of having a foot in both camps in that they are sometimes part of the Scrum but also a part of the business proper. This means that they might not have overall responsibility for the delivery of requirements by the team, as the needs of the business might sway them. The business might need to act in an agile manner in response to changes in the market, which would mean the product owner being given priorities by their organisational structure and subsequently upsetting the original roadmap. The product owner's ability to think strategically is essential, and they must also have an appreciation that 'no plan survives contact with the enemy' (paraphrased in Barnett, 1963, p. 35). This appreciation of strategy should be fostered among all members of the team, though.

Designer

The product owner role is related to that of the designer, in that they not only work closely together to provide a blueprint for the final solution but are also people that a front-end developer might communicate with by bypassing the Scrum master.

The primary distinction between front-end developers and designers can be described in terms of a map and the territory it depicts (Wilson, 1977). The designer is the cartographer responsible for mapping the user journey and the things that they will see on that journey; the front-end developer is responsible for building the terrain. The designer is likely to use different tools to the front-end developer. It used to be that the tools employed by designers, such as 'what you see is what you get' (WYSIWYG, pronounced 'wizz-ee-wig') tools, were popular. However, the markup these generated was often notoriously difficult to read as it was convoluted and just plain messy,[8] so they lost favour with front-end developers, who instead chose to hand-craft the markup and CSS.

One such program, Microsoft's Sketch2Code (Microsoft, 2018), might make an impact on your future career as a front-end developer. Thanks to the vagaries of Internet Explorer 11, there will still be a place for front-end developers for quite some time to come.

---

[8] As we will see later, there are many ways of generating markup that appears the same to the end user. Not all these ways are as desirable as others – for instance, embedding styling within attributes of HTML is best avoided. This type of code is often called 'spaghetti code' and can be difficult for other developers to change later.

While designers and front-end developers have a similar appreciation of the look of an application, I have found that a designer sometimes cannot understand all the limitations of the 'canvas' which will be used. I have had conversations with designers about styling select inputs – where a user is asked to choose one or more options – and whether it is possible to style the different options in different ways. It is possible, but users are familiar with the mechanism of select inputs, so I dissuaded designers from styling them in a way that might lead to cognitive dissonance.

Your working relationship with the designer on your team, if there is one, is likely to be as close as that with the back-end or full-stack developers on your team. To an extent, you act as a mediator between the aesthetics and the mechanism of the application; you help to display information in a pleasing manner which does not disguise its importance. The designer will have spent time thinking about this process and will likely have specialist skills in areas such as user interface (UI) or user experience (UX), so it is worth following their thought processes. This understanding of their thought processes will not only aid your users' journey but will also help you in the future when you might not have access to such a resource.

As a front-end developer, you should be aware of current design trends and how they will affect you – because they will: when your employer gets excited by a trend and asks you to implement it, or when you spot something which will enhance your users' experience on their journey through the application you are crafting. A designer is likely to be involved in the creation of these trends.

17

Quality assurance

Quality assurance (QA) team members can be both the bane and the delight of your life. They are responsible for testing the things that you develop.

I asked Annie dela Cruz, one of my QA colleagues, to describe her role, and this is what she said:

Firstly, QAs need to make sure that the implemented software or application is based on business requirements and that it is working as expected – that's the main thing. Secondly, QAs need to make sure that the application is usable, that negative inputs will return messages for the user, and that overall design, usability, compatibility and integration with other systems are all working as expected.

It is always entertaining to look at a test system after a QA has done their work, as there will be all kinds of oddness, with user inputs filled with random bits of JavaScript or image tags to ensure that the system can cope with people attempting to inject malicious code into it.

Here's a funny QA joke, which might have originated with Bill Sempf (2014). It illustrates the sorts of tests to which a QA might subject your work:

QA Engineer walks into a bar. Orders a beer. Orders 0 beers. Orders 999999999 beers. Orders a lizard. Orders −1 beers. Orders a sfdeljknesv.

Depending upon the organisation of your team, QA professionals may well be part of your stand-up meeting, and it is worth spending time developing a relationship with them. Being comfortable with them will mean that you can gain a greater understanding of any bugs they identify.

They are certainly not the only people who should test your work. Testing is one of the responsibilities of front-end developers so you should ideally test everything you change in all browsers you support before making a pull request, then ask another developer to review your pull request. Should your changes pass this cursory inspection, you should then ask another developer to test them in whatever test system you have before letting the QA loose. Following this process, or at least something similar, helps to prevent your users from being tripped up by something that you have written.

SUMMARY

Front-end developers are crucial to modern businesses. Without an attractive and functional website, potential clients will look elsewhere. Moreover, when it comes to production applications, a poorly presented and difficult-to-use application will see existing customers leaving to use a competitor's application; even if it offers less functionality, if it is more engaging they will prefer it. You owe it to yourself to ensure that your hard work is presented as well as possible to as broad an audience as possible. Quite apart from anything else, a well-presented website or application will engender trust.

Front-end developers need to foster many soft and hard skills to become competent practitioners, and we will discuss these tools in the next chapter. The volume of tools can seem daunting, but please do not be disheartened, as front-end development is an immensely rewarding career. And those skills will find utility in other areas of your personal and professional life as well.

2 TOOLS OF THE TRADE

In this chapter, we will examine the primary tools you should be aware of and familiar with as a front-end developer.

PRIMARY TOOLS

Fire is only possible if oxygen, heat and fuel are present. Similarly, in order to have some measure of professional competence, the front-end developer must have some degree of familiarity with each of the following three technologies: Hypertext Markup Language (HTML), Cascading Style Sheets (CSS)[1] and JavaScript. These form the front-end developer triangle, pictured in Figure 2.1. This first section of the chapter details each of these technologies in turn.

Figure 2.1 Front-end developer triangle

---

1 While HTML allows for some basic styling conventions, such as making a heading appear different from the content of the application, we can get much more fine-grained control using CSS.

To properly understand the importance of HTML, CSS and JavaScript, some understanding of browsers is required. All browsers share similar functionality in that they:

- **Fetch data:** a dedicated network layer fetches data from web servers via the internet.

- **Process data:** the network layer passes the data to several processing subsystems.

- **Display data:** once processed, the data is displayed to the user.

- **Store data:** some information needs to be stored, and several mechanisms are available for this purpose.

Further, the processing and display of the data can be broken down even more:

- **The rendering engine:** generates the render tree from parsed HTML and CSS.

- **The JavaScript engine:** reads and converts into machine code any JavaScript present.

- **The UI back-end:** 'paints' the product generated by the rendering engine.

The first of these, the rendering engine, is where the first two of our three technologies – HTML and CSS – are processed. The HTML is parsed to create the document object model (DOM) tree, while all CSS is parsed to create a CSS object model (CSSOM) tree. The DOM and CSSOM trees are then combined to generate a render tree, which represents a tree of styled DOM nodes. It is at this point that the browser knows where things should appear on the device displaying the processed data – that is, where items should appear on the rendered page. A rather gruesome analogy would be between a skull and a face: on its own the DOM represents the skeleton of what we will eventually see. It is only when we add the musculature, flesh and skin represented by the CSSOM that the final figure becomes clear. The render tree is not presented to the UI back-end in one chunk of data; instead, the rendering process passes processed data piecemeal, as and when the networking layer has fetched the data and the data has been processed; thus, the UI back-end optimistically paints the contents of the page as they are processed – it takes a best guess at rendering the content, which can sometimes mean that the layout changes as more HTML and CSS is processed.

JavaScript can interrupt the rendering engine if it is contained in an inline script element within the HTML, at which point the JavaScript engine executes the JavaScript before again allowing the rendering engine to continue with its work.

Should the JavaScript element have a reference to an external file, then the JavaScript will be fetched by the networking layer. Once it arrives, it will be processed by the JavaScript engine. Once the JavaScript engine has finished processing the retrieved JavaScript, the rendering engine continues parsing the rest of the HTML.

There are significant benefits of having the script inline as there is less of a delay to the rendering engine if the JavaScript requested is already within the page and does not require fetching. However, JavaScript files can be large and so it is now the common preferred practice for external JavaScript files to be referenced at the bottom of the page to allow the rendering engine to get on with its primary task without interruptions.

You might be wondering why the JavaScript engine can interrupt the vital business of the rendering engine. This delay is required because JavaScript can be employed to interact with the DOM and CSSOM of the page. In such cases, there would be little point parsing and rendering HTML and CSS as it might then be affected by the processed JavaScript. In other words, it makes sense for the browser to give priority to JavaScript over HTML and CSS – though it is worthwhile noting that CSS can block the JavaScript engine, as the browser understands that the JavaScript can alter the CSSOM, so it will need to be in place before the JavaScript can interact with it.

This is a simplistic overview of how browsers work. There are different types of browser, and they all have slightly different ways of working with HTML, CSS and JavaScript.

Ensure you place your JavaScript just before the closing body element of any pages you create so that the HTML and CSS are processed and rendered without any delay caused by downloading and processing JavaScript. This will also ensure that any JavaScript that alters either the DOM or the CSSOM has something to work with.

HTML

For the front-end developer, HTML (Hypertext Markup Language) is both the canvas and the paint which we use. If we have no understanding of the medium in which we work, we are left not being able to use all the tools we have at our disposal, and that would be a waste, as HTML is a remarkable language.

When I began learning systems analysis and design, the tutors on my course asked about languages we had used and all sorts were mentioned, such as Pascal, C and C++, and I think there was even mention of C#. I admitted I knew nothing to any great depth, as I had been a practising nurse, but I do remember the subtle chuckle which was prompted by someone answering 'HTML'.

At the time I did not clock the issue, which is that HTML is not classed as a 'proper' programming language and is instead seen as a markup language (although I am pretty sure my lecturers said that it was a valid answer). A markup language is one in which information has structure. The markup allows the device rendering the information to receive hidden instructions regarding its layout, without those instructions generally being seen by the reader. I didn't know enough to argue, but I did remember my wife of the time coming back from university some time previously and waxing lyrical about this new technology called HTML, and the opportunities it offered for exploring language in the context of literature (she was undertaking a combined English and women's studies degree).

So, I went off and tried to learn it myself and got distracted by its precursor – XML – and down I fell, lost in the rabbit hole.

Initially developed by Tim Berners-Lee in 1989 while he was working at CERN, HTML was designed to allow academics to share papers on the early internet, having roots some 20 years further back.

I mentioned the DOM tree earlier, but how should we imagine it? You can try to imagine it as a real tree, though that is not entirely appropriate, as it's more of an inverted tree or the root system of a tree – a sort of organogram, hierarchy or family tree (as shown in Figure 2.2). In this way, a DOM tree can be represented as a sort of branching structure with elements spreading out to many ultimate termini. Each part or node of the page represents an element within a hierarchy.

HTML is the trunk which encapsulates the boughs; the boughs then encapsulate the branches, the branches encapsulate the twigs and the twigs encapsulate the leaves.

The trunk of the tree that is any web page is the `html` element (the markup is made up of 'elements', but you will also see them referred to as 'tags'). It is the most crucial part of a web page but also the part most often ignored. It is primarily important because along with the document type definition it tells the browser how to interpret the contents of the page.

Figure 2.2 A simple DOM tree

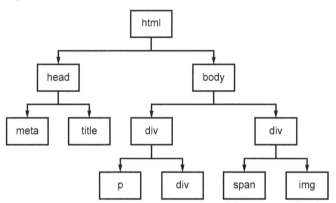

A document type definition (DTD) is a document that defines the structure of the HTML document – the web page or application – and any associated rules. It was primarily important in documents written before HTML5 (the most recent version of HTML at the time of writing), as they were based on an older language called Standard Generalized Markup Language (SGML) and were invalid without a DTD.

The DTD is referred to in the very first element of an HTML document, even before the **html** element. Before HTML5, it contained four declarations:

- the root element – for HTML documents this would be **html**;

- the type of DTD to be referenced – usually **PUBLIC** in the case of HTML;

- the formal public identifier (FPI) of the DTD – used to identify a specification uniquely;

- the final part, the uniform resource locator (URL) – the location of the DTD.

You will likely only ever see this form of **doctype** element, rather than being asked to write HTML in anything other than HTML5. HTML5 is no longer related to SGML and so has one declaration, as you can see in the skeleton code below. It is important to understand the other forms of **doctypes**, though, as this will allow you to understand what previous developers were aiming to produce when you look over their work.

There are only two boughs coming from the trunk represented by the **html** element, but everything else hangs from those two boughs. They are the **head** and **body** elements.

Traditionally, the body is where most of the content of the web page resides, with the head element being something of a stub, usually only used to provide information for the browser and tell it where to get any CSS associated with the page and to hold other metadata (data about data). Metadata is not displayed to the user, but the head element also contains the title of the document, which is presented to the user within the tab of the page. Metadata can tell the browser which character set the document should use as well as a whole list of other information, such as the keywords for search engines and information about the author of the page.

At its most basic, this suffices as an HTML page:

```
<!doctype html>
<html lang="en">
    <head>
        <meta charset="utf-8">
        <title>HTML Template</title>
    </head>
    <body>
        <p>A paragraph</p>
    </body>
</html>
```

Producing this within a browser gives the result shown in Figure 2.3.

Figure 2.3 A basic HTML template reproduced in a browser

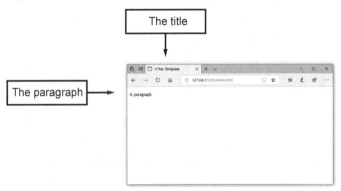

We have talked about elements but what do we mean by that? Let's flesh out the HTML above.

Anatomy of HTML

HTML elements are simply one or more characters surrounded by angle brackets. When we look at the content of the **body** element above, we can see a paragraph element (**p**) with some text within it. The text is the content of the element and is surrounded by an opening tag and a closing tag – we know it is a closing tag because it has the slash character (**/**) preceding the name of the element.

As we can see from the HTML above, elements can contain other elements in the same way that the **html** element contains the **body** element and the **body** element includes the **p** (paragraph) element. Further, all HTML elements can have attributes. We will now examine these structures a little more.

Attributes The example above is quite simple, and the only elements which have attributes are **html** and **meta**.

27

If we go back to the tree analogy, we have a set of nested containers (tree, bough, branch, twig and leaf), but what if we want to say something that is a quality of the containing element? HTML borrows a mechanism from XML and uses attributes. Attributes such as **lang** in our opening **html**, or **charset** in the **meta** element, tell the browser that we are presenting it with an HTML document written in English (**en**) using the **utf-8** character set. Here we say that the **html** element has the name of **lang** and the value of **en** and the **meta** element has the name of **charset** with a value of **utf-8**. As you can tell, attributes are most often made up of name–value pairs, but some attributes simply have a name.

The code below is the same as the example above but with different formatting: the attributes are displayed on new lines underneath their elements. Such formatting can be make the parsing of markup easier, especially if there are many attributes and also if the document is very long and complex. I use similar formatting myself as it makes navigating the code much simpler and allows me to see at a glance the attributes and their values.

```
<!doctype html>
<html
    lang="en">
    <head>
        <meta
            charset="utf-8">
        <title>HTML Template</title>
    </head>
    <body>
        <p>A paragraph</p>
    </body>
</html>
```

Attributes are vital to HTML. They are one of the more powerful parts of the language, and there are even some elements which have little or no use without attributes, most notably the **img** element, which embeds an image in the HTML (images are discussed later in this chapter). Most attributes have a value, while some affect their element merely by being present (W3C, 1991).

Indentation Looking back at the code above, within most editors, you will see the same structure formatted like this:

```
<!doctype html>
<html lang="en">
<head>
    <meta charset="utf-8">
    <title>HTML Template</title>
</head>
<body>
    <p>A paragraph</p>
</body>
</html>
```

This formatting places the **head** and **body** elements at the same level of the hierarchy as the **html** element, but this misrepresents its philosophical importance within the structure. Another thing to note is the indentation, and this is something every developer will appreciate. Improperly indented code is unhelpful and can lead to mistakes, and even the method of indentation can be problematic.

An exciting revelation from the Stack Overflow 2017 Developer Survey was that there are financial implications associated with the choice of indentation (Robinson, 2017). The results of the survey showed that those developers who care little about the mechanism of indentation – those developers who, so long as the indentation 'looks' correct, are happy to use a mixture of tabs and spaces – earn less than those who are consistent with their method of indentation, be it tabs or spaces. It might be supposed that the lack of consistency this approach represents raises concerns among employers.

When we look at the markup code above, we can parse it merely by scanning down the page; we see the vertical wave, and that wave becomes increasingly complex the more extensive the document and the higher the number of nested elements.

> What happens when we put many attributes on the same element? Depending on the editor or integrated development environment (IDE) used, there will be some line breaks or lines will break out of the nominal 80-character limit, or even off the side of the screen. The 80-character limit is historical and arose from the original width of the IBM Punch Card (Coster, 2012), but it is worth bearing in mind as, even though it is arbitrary, it is a convention.

One way of solving this issue is to use the same indentation for the attributes of the element as is used for the children of that element (i.e. those elements which are contained within it in the hierarchy). However, personally, I find that aesthetically unpleasing in that it misrepresents the hierarchy. Such a form of gross indentation is what I have illustrated above, but the jarring gap between the **html** and **meta** elements and their children does not help with understanding the visual flow of the markup. Instead, I prefer to use two spaces between the start of the element and its attributes so that there is a subtler distinction and then use four spaces between nested elements. Thus the above snippet could be presented like this:

```
<!doctype html>
<html
  lang="en">
    <head>
        <meta
          charset="utf-8">
        <title>HTML Template</title>
    </head>
    <body>
        <p>A paragraph</p>
    </body>
</html>
```

Such indentation is going overboard, though, and is not required unless lines are likely to break the 80-character limit.

This approach to indentation is one of the preferred HTML line-wrapping styles in the *Google HTML/CSS Style Guide* (Google, 2018). Reading style guides can be worthwhile, not least because they generally offer justification for the decisions made; such arguments can inform your practice.

Structure of HTML

We now understand the nature of HTML elements, so next we will look at some common elements which you will see as a front-end developer. In the example we have been looking at above, we only have two elements with any substance, the `title` element and the `p` (paragraph) element.

As mentioned earlier, HTML was first used to share academic papers over the nascent internet. Its primary purpose was the display of written information, so it makes sense that Tim Berners-Lee shortened the **paragraph** element to a single `p`. In text rich documents, this is likely to be used extensively.

I have noted that HTML elements can contain other elements and that those elements, such as the `p` element, can contain further elements, such as **span** elements (see below). Such nesting allows children to inherit behaviour and styling from their parent elements.

A full discussion of all the elements of HTML is beyond this book, but a simple examination of the basics follows.

Headings   HTML provides six levels of heading (**h1** through to **h6**) for use in the separation of content in much the same way as headlines are used in newspapers to attract the attention of the reader or describe the content, and lower levels of heading are used to highlight less important content. The **h1** element is used for the primary heading, and, in much the same way as there is only ever one main newspaper headline, an HTML document should only have one **h1** element. Each browser will display them in similar ways with increasingly smaller text but all in bold text and with margins.

Division   The division (**div**) element is the primary container for other elements and can contain any other text or HTML element. It is a block-level element, which means that by default browsers place a line break before and after the element. A **div** element commonly has an **id** attribute, which allows it to be identified for CSS styling or JavaScript manipulation. Such **id** attributes must be unique within the page to ensure that the target is individual. Should you wish to target multiple elements, then the **class** attribute does not have the same restriction of uniqueness. Both **id** and **class** can be present in an element's opening tag.

Span   Unlike the **div** element, the span element is displayed inline with no break above or beneath by default. The **span** element typically contains short pieces of text or other HTML elements which need to be separated from the main body of the containing element.

Other inline elements   Like the span element, there are two further inline elements which can separate content from the containing element but are primarily used for styling text. These two elements are the **em** (standing for 'emphasis') and **strong** elements. The **em** element generally renders its child text as italic, and the **strong** element presents it as bold. A further inline element is a line break (**br**), which is used to force a line break within the body of the text. The **br** is one inline element that does not have to include a closing tag.

Lists Lists allow the display of information in one of two ways, either through the use of a numbered list (using an `ol` element) or through the use of bullets in no particular order (using a `ul` element). Each type of list contains a set of items identified using the `li` element. The usage of the `ol` and `ul` elements is similar but different: you can think of the `li` elements of an `ol` element being a sequence and the `li` elements of the `ul` as a set of elements in no particular order. The choice of whether you use a `ul` or `ol` is dependent upon whether or not the order of the child `li` elements is important.

Images The `img` element is one element that relies upon its attributes. The `img` element is self-closing in that it has an opening tag but no closing tag; instead, it has a slash preceding the final angle bracket. The `img` element must have a source (`src`) attribute set to the URL of an image. This example of a simple `img` element is taken from MDN Web Docs (formerly Mozilla Developer Network) (Mozilla, 2020f):

```
<img src="mdn-logo-sm.png" alt="MDN" />
```

Here we can see that we are asking the browser to display an image saved as 'mdn-logo-sm.png', which is in the PNG (portable network graphics) format. Further, the image has an alternative attribute (`alt`) of 'MDN', which will be displayed if the image link fails or the image has not yet been retrieved.

> The `alt` attribute, along with some other attributes, such as `title` and `longdesc`, is essential for users who have visual impairments, but do please check the MDN document for further aids to accessibility (Mozilla, 2020f). Along with these standard HTML attributes, the Web Accessibility Initiative has developed some Accessible Rich Internet Application (AWI-ARIA or ARIA) attributes, which warrant far greater discussion than can be provided within this book.

While I prefer to make both **img** and **br** elements self-closing, HTML5 has removed such directives, and you will see them both with and without a slash before the final angle bracket.

Another element which, in my opinion, warrants self-closing is the **input** element, but this is again a stylistic choice. We will examine **input** elements in far greater detail in Chapter 3 when we examine forms but, as might be surmised from their name, they allow users to enter data in an application. I prefer these elements to be self-closing as it merely feels more complete.

Opinionated practices are rife in all areas of development and throughout human endeavour. If you do not agree with mine, please develop your own, but do bear in mind that you are signing your work whenever you do.

Videos   We are now no longer limited to displaying images within HTML documents and can make use of videos. They share the **src** attribute but are not self-closing as their text content is presented to the viewer if the format of the video is not supported or if the video fails to load, acting a little like the **alt** attribute of the image. Videos can also have **width**, **height** and **controls** attributes, with the **controls** attribute defining whether or not the browser should display video controls such as 'play' and 'pause'.

HTML summary
The above are some of the most common HTML elements. There are many more and their number is increasing, so do keep abreast of developments. A wider discussion of HTML is beyond the scope of this book, but do spend some time reading around the subject – it is fascinating.

As you journey through your career, you will start to appreciate that there are many ways to accomplish the same thing. Despite the constant trend towards managers being desirous of conformity, individual developers all have their style.

I have had opportunities to appreciate this, especially when seeking out a developer in a team to ask for clarification. I often find that I know just whom to approach because I recognise their style of coding.

In terms of where your HTML will be displayed, it must be noted that trends are always in a state of flux, with screen sizes increasing on the desktop but fluctuating massively elsewhere. As such, we must take a little time to think about the users' journey and navigation around our work. We cannot trust that keeping the user limited to a screen height will allow even the most straightforward headline to be displayed appropriately – we might have banners or menus at the top of the screen which will make the headline appear out of the current view when the page loads.

CSS

In this section, we will examine Cascading Style Sheets (CSS). To borrow an analogy from the military: when an officer tells you to jump, it is the sergeant who tells you how high. In this case, the HTML is an instruction to the browser (the officer) and the CSS is the modifier which details the presentation of the direction (the sergeant). Put another way: the HTML is the structure and the CSS details how the structure should be presented.

While HTML deals with the structure and content of the page and allows some limited formatting of that data, using HTML on its own offers very little control over that formatting. Each browser implements limited styling using its built-in stylesheets, called 'user agent stylesheets' (Meiert, 2007), but each browser manufacturer has slightly different thoughts about how specific elements should be displayed. No plain HTML file is presented in the same way in different browsers, and sometimes not even between different versions of the same browser.

Tim Berners-Lee and others initially saw HTML's lack of formatting control as a good thing because HTML was deemed to be a language for the publication of documents on the internet and nothing else. Abilities that were available in word processors of the time were not supported – changing the typeface, colour or any other aspect of the presentation was not possible.

While it may have been enough for academics to have minimal control over the final rendering of a page, the web was becoming more popular. Businesses and designers were far more conscious of their image, preferring not to let software manufacturers dictate how their presence on the web be displayed.

The original specification of CSS was called 'Cascading HTML Style Sheets' (Lie, 1994), suggesting that it might be used in other markup languages. Along with the control that CSS offered in conjunction with user agent stylesheets, it was thought that the user might want to dictate how the page would appear and override the user agent stylesheet[2] and the author.

Once it had been standardised, CSS quickly took off as a way of styling HTML documents.

Anatomy of CSS
CSS works by breaking up styling declarations into rules, with each rule consisting of a selector and a declaration block.

---

2   The 'user agent stylesheet' is the default set of styles within a browser. They dictate the appearance of markup when there is no CSS within a page.

What that means in practical terms is that each element in an HTML document can be selected and rules applied to that selector. A selector can be a common element such as a single paragraph (**p**), a subset of all paragraphs with a specific **class** or a particular paragraph identified with a unique **id** attribute. The following rules, for instance, target all paragraphs, paragraphs with a **class** (**emphasis**) and a single paragraph (with the **id** of **recently-deleted**):

```
p {
    color: red;
}
p.emphasis {
    font-weight: bold;
}
p#recently-deleted {
    text-decoration: line-through;
}
```

In the example above, we can see that a period indicates a **class** and a hashtag indicates an **id**. To go a little deeper, we are saying that all **p** elements should have a **color** of **red**, those **p** elements which have a **class** of **emphasis** should have a **font-weight**[3] of **bold**, and the **p** element with an **id** of **recently-deleted** should have a **text-decoration** of **line-through**.

Note that you will be unlikely to see such specific selectors when you examine CSS files, as it is unusual for the selector to be so precise.

This HTML illustrates the concept:

```
<p>This should be red</p>
<p class="emphasis">
    This should be red and bold
</p>
```

---

3 A discussion of all CSS properties and their associated values is beyond the scope of this book, but there are excellent introductions provided by W3Schools (2020b) and MDN Web Docs (Mozilla, 2020c).

```
<p class="emphasis"
    id="recently-deleted">
    This paragraph should be
    red, bold and there should
    be a line throught it.
</p>
```

The CSS declaration block is made up of one or more declarations, which are property–value pairs separated by semicolons enclosed within braces. To return to our military analogy, the order to jump is the property, but the value is how high. To return to the HTML tree analogy in the previous section, the CSS tells us how the tree should look – the shade of the leaves and the texture of the bark, if you will.

In the CSS example above, we are targeting all paragraphs with a **class** of **emphasis** in our second rule. However, if we wanted all heading elements with a **class** of **emphasis**, we would need to duplicate the rules for each heading element (**h1**, **h2**, **h3**, **h4**, **h5** and **h6**). Rather than duplicate the same rule for similar classes, we can instead select all elements with the **class** of **emphasis** by removing the **p** from the declaration, thus making our rule less targeted:

```
.emphasis {
    font-weight: bold;
}
```

To return once again to our tree analogy, the DOM represents one tree whereas the CSSOM represents a similar tree which mirrors some or all parts of the DOM tree. According to the analogy provided earlier, HTML is the skull and CSS is the flesh and skin that sit atop the skull.

The cascade

The term 'Cascading Style Sheet' warrants exploration. 'Style Sheet' suggests an external document separate from the HTML document, but this is not always the case: CSS can be an external document referred to in the head of the HTML document using a **link** element:

```
<link rel="stylesheet" type="text/css" href="style.css">
```

Here we see that the **link** element has three attributes:

- the **rel** attribute, which specifies the relationship between the current document and the linked document (the example above tells the browser to create a link between the document and a **stylesheet**);

- the **type** attribute, which instructs the browser to expect that the stylesheet will be in the media type of **text/css**;

- the **href** attribute, which specifies the URL of the document.

Alternatively, it is possible to embed the CSS within the **head** element of the HTML within a **style** element. Putting a style declaration within the head increases the size of the initial document, though, and if you wish to use the same styles in different documents, you have to duplicate the **style** element. This means that if a style needs to be changed, all instances of the **style** element must be edited.

CSS can also be used directly in the element using a **style** attribute:

```
<p style="color: red; font-weight: bold;">
    This should be red and bold
</p>
```

This kind of use of CSS is called 'inline CSS'. It can be useful, but it loses many of the advantages of CSS, as it mixes the content with the presentation. It should therefore be avoided or used sparingly.

I recently came across a problem where I had to add CSS dynamically via JavaScript in order for a matrix to change dimensions. This was unavoidable, but it was limited to only those aspects which would change, as the main style was dictated in an external CSS file.

We have looked at the three ways of including CSS because doing so illustrates the term 'cascading'. The final styling for a document depends on where the rules are: external, internal (within a style element) or inline. The source matters: inline styles have precedence over external and internal styles, and internal rules have greater priority than external styles. Further, rules loaded later have precedence over earlier rules; this means that if rules are loaded from multiple external sources, then the final source referenced within the head takes precedence. That is to say, if we load two external stylesheets with different rules for styling a specific element, the last takes precedence over the first.

There are further principles regarding the specificity of the rules, with more specific being applied over generic rules. To expand on this further: if we have multiple elements all styled a specific way but one has a class, then styles associated with the class will be applied rather than the generic styling. We saw an example of this when we looked at the styling of three paragraph elements earlier.

Chaining or extending

At the beginning of this section we looked at an example of adding an `emphasis class` to some elements, but what if we wanted to make one of these elements italic as well as bold? We could write a new CSS rule called `emphasis-italic` or instead create another `class` called `italic`. This distinction illustrates the difference between chaining and extending a `class`; instead of extending the `emphasis class` to style the text italic, we instead chain another `class` which makes the text italic.

Using the modular technique of chaining means that your CSS codebase is kept clean, and you can give your classes names that are appropriate to what they do, which makes it easier to keep track of them. It can cause something called 'class madness'[4] – but in practice it is easy to maintain such

---

[4] 'Class madness' is a term used by Sarah Dayan in a discussion of chaining or extending CSS classes (Dayan, 2018). She notes that the use of chaining can lead to very many classes being added to elements.

a naming system, and it might be something you'll thank yourself for later.

Extending classes makes for far more readable and clutter-free HTML, but the CSS can become much more cumbersome. Sarah Dayan (2018) offers some thoughts about the issues of chaining and extending extensively, with examples and arguments for and against each approach. Whichever you choose, it's important to understand both and to implement them consistently and sensibly. I appreciate a well-named class that tells me just what it does, be that an element having a class attribute having a value of **emphasis-italic** or **emphasis** and **italic**. To give an example in code, this shows how to extend a class:

```
<div class="emphasis-italic">Some bold and italic text
styled by extending the emphasis class</div>
```

Whereas this shows class chaining:

```
<div class="emphasis italic">Some bold and italic text
styled by adding two separate classes</div>
```

CSS toolchain

Modern CSS can be written in other dialects, such as Stylus or Syntactically Awesome Style Sheets (SASS). There are many such dialects that promise to make writing CSS more manageable, though there is something of a learning curve involved and recent changes to CSS (such as custom properties – sometimes referred to as 'CSS variables') are making their use less relevant. These dialects are called 'pre-processors', and once they have outputted the desired CSS it is often piped through an auto-prefixer[5] post-processor, to ensure that even

---

5 A prefix is sometimes added to a CSS property by a browser so that the browser can start to support experimental CSS declarations. Each vendor has a different one, with WebKit (used by Chrome, Safari, newer versions of Opera and the default Android browser) using **-webkit**, Firefox using **-moz**, older (pre-WebKit) Opera using **-o** and Internet Explorer using **-ms**. An auto-prefixer takes the experimental property and duplicates it four times, prepends the relevant prefix to take into account all of these browsers, and inserts the resulting code above the original rule.

though the developer has written CSS3,[6] it will work across all browsers which support the CSS module.

These steps between the writing of the original CSS in a dialect and the final CSS lead to the term 'toolchain'. The dialect is converted into idealised CSS, which should work in a world of standards-compliant browsers, and then the relevant prefixes are added. Sometimes, too, whole new rules are written for specific features on older browsers (for instance, Internet Explorer 11 has an older implementation of grid layout, and some auto-prefixers are smart enough to generate the appropriate CSS for you). This multistep process is known as a toolchain, and we will learn about other toolchains when we explore JavaScript later in this chapter.

CSS measurement units

To an extent, there are two general types of CSS measurements: those which are characterised as fixed and those which are characterised as relative. There is significant debate about which kind is preferred among developers.

Absolute units   We have absolute (sometimes also called 'fixed') units of measurement, such as `cm`, `mm`, `Q`, `in`, `pt`, `pc` and `px`. But even these can be different across devices:

- `cm` is a measurement in centimetres.

- `mm` is a measurement in millimetres.

- `Q` is a measurement in quarter-millimetres.

- `in` is a measurement in inches.

- `pt` is a measurement in points, with there being 72 points in an inch.

- `pc` is a measurement in picas, with a pica being 12 points, meaning that there are 6 picas per inch.

- `px` is a measurement in pixels.

---

6   See the summary of this section below for an explanation of CSS3.

Most of these measurements are absolute, in that neither the imperial nor the decimal measurements are subject to change. This is not the case with pixels, though, as pixel density is increasing all the time.

USING PIXELS (PX) AND POINTS (PT)

Pixel density is measured using either pixels per inch (PPI) or pixels per centimetre (PPCM) and is calculated from the diagonal size of the screen and the resolution of the screen in pixels. This variety explains why displays are often described using their diagonal size (Tyson & Carmack, 2000). The size of a pixel is not guaranteed to be the same across all the devices your users will be working on, so why are they used?

Design software such as Photoshop defaults to using pixels as a unit of measurement, so designers use them in the designs passed to front-end developers (if designers are involved; they are more prevalent in larger projects). Front-end developers understand pixels because they are closely associated with what they see all day during their practice. Thus, they represent a point of contact between designers and front-end developers.

Despite pixels being a measure shared by two members of the development team, the user is unlikely to be overly concerned with them, excepting that they might be persuaded to buy a device with a higher number of pixels per inch over another product, thanks to the perceived benefit of higher pixel density. There are accessibility concerns with using the pixel though.

Using pixels as your preferred measure can lead to unforeseen consequences, especially when a user alters their default font size. Imagine a user setting their font size to be significantly larger than the 16px default when you have created **header** elements with a restricted

43

size. This change would dramatically impact the appearance of the final product. As discussed in Chapter 1, accessibility should not be something you merely consider at the end of your work process but should be at the forefront of everything you do. While the pixel does not scale upwards for visually impaired users, neither does it scale downwards very well for users working on mobile devices.

The **point** is the smallest unit of measurement in typography, and it is still used extensively within the world of desktop publishing. For example, Microsoft Word uses it as a measure for the height of all its fonts. Points suffer from the same restrictions as pixels, though. Moreover, they originate in the world of print media, which is very different from digital, with this divergence only growing wider.

Both pixels and points should be used with caution and with an understanding that their deployment should be examined for any impact on accessibility.

Relative units So much for the absolute measurements. What are the relative units of measurement?

- `%` is a measurement as a percentage relative to another element, usually its parent.

- One `em` is the height of the font (it is based on the width of the uppercase letter M, which is generally as wide as it is tall).

- One `rem` is the height of the font size of the root element of an HTML document.

- One `ch` is the width of the 0 (zero) character.

- One `ex` is the height of a lowercase x in a typeface.

- One **vh** is 1% of a viewport's height.[7]
- One **vw** is 1% of a viewport's width.
- One **vmin** is 1% of a viewport's height or width (whichever is the smaller value).
- One **vmax** is 1% of a viewport's height or width (whichever is the higher value).
- One **fr** represents a fraction of the leftover space in a grid container (see Chapter 3 for more on grid layouts).

The units **em** and **rem** are closely related, but it is easy to get them confused and easy to get in trouble with nested elements, as the **em** takes its parent element as the reference when its size is calculated. While this can be useful when we know we want a child element to display at a different size to its parent, it can get confusing when using such relative units, especially in deeply nested elements, such as ordered or unordered lists (**ol** or **ul** elements, respectively). I have come a cropper with this myself so I fully appreciate the **rem**, as it does not change relative to any container other than the root element. Using this unit also means that to adjust the size of all elements within a document, we can change the size of the root element.

Similarly, **ch** and **ex** are related in that they are concerned with the measurement of specific characters, but, even then, these can be different across different typefaces and are thus determined by the **font-family** directive within a document's CSS. The **ch** unit is not as well supported as the **ex** unit and, according to Jonathan Cutrell (2014), the **ex** unit's primary usage is for micro-adjustments of typography, with Stephen Poley (2013) suggesting it could be ignored completely.

The **vh**, **vw**, **vmin** and **vmax** units are all associated with the viewport being used by our users and as such should be things we consider.

---

[7] The viewport, in this context, is the area taken up by the browser window. When the browser is in full-screen mode on a desktop or laptop computer, this is the whole size of the monitor used. In the case of mobile phones or tablets, this is most often the size of the display – though, taking into account that a phone might be rotated 90°, this might be either portrait of landscape.

> I have found the **vh**, **vw**, **vmin** and **vmax** units immensely useful when using Grid-layouts to ensure that the text within those elements fits, depending on the resolution of the screen.

It has been pointed out that similar effects can be achieved using media queries (which we will look at next). However, to make the exact same effect, media queries would need to be duplicated multiple times whereas using viewport units means that 'when the height or width of the initial containing block is changed, they are scaled accordingly' (W3C, 2018).

Regarding the **fr** unit, it is worth noting that it can be mixed with other units of measurement when using Grid layouts, allowing us to define fixed widths and heights and allowing the browser to fill in the remaining fractions of space.

Then there is the percentage measurement, which is especially useful in conjunction with the **calc** (Mozilla, 2020a) CSS function (explored further below). It is like the viewport units, but there are some caveats, as the width of the **body** element (as a percentage) does not considering any margin. The viewport units have warnings too, as issues can arise with any scrollbars which are present on the page.

Both absolute and relative measurement units have their place. While I have briefly touched on the debate between the different camps, you will doubtless see much more of these arguments while researching your work. It is essential to understand what each unit means, but it is also important to consider your aesthetic principles. I would suggest that relative units are particularly important when considering typography and general layouts, but absolute units can be useful in their place, such as for print layouts where the output medium is known. The front-end developer is in a conflicted world and needs to understand both absolute and relative elements, as will be seen in greater depth when we examine images in the next chapter and look at the differences between raster and vector images.

CSS media queries

I suggested above that media queries can fulfil the same role as viewport units but that we might find ourselves duplicating CSS declarations with only small changes between each media query. But what do I mean by media queries?

Media queries were suggested by Lie as part of the original CSS proposal in 1994, but they did not make it into the specification until 2001 and were only correctly supported in 2012. They do not look like regular CSS but rather enclose CSS, with that enclosed CSS only being used when the media query returns true. They are made up of a media type and one or more expressions. More often than not that media type will be **screen** for front-end developers, unless you are asked to develop specific styling for printing – in which case you will want the **print** media type.

The expressions involve querying media features, and it is worth looking at least at the width feature, which details the width of the rendering surface, as it is used to check the width of the device accessing the application or website and so can be used to alter the styles used by the browser, depending on the device. The following example, from W3Schools,[8] illustrates a typical use case for media queries:

```
/* Set the background color of body to tan */
body {
  background-color: tan;
}

/* On screens that are 992px or less, set the
background color to blue */
@media screen and (max-width: 992px) {
  body {
    background-color: blue;
  }
}
```

---

8 https://www.w3schools.com/css/tryit.asp?filename=trycss_mediaqueries_ex1.

```
/* On screens that are 600px or less, set the
background color to olive */
@media screen and (max-width: 600px) {
  body {
    background-color: olive;
  }
}
```

While changing the background colour of the **body** element depending on the width of the screen, as in the code above, is not a usual requirement, the numbers above are ones that might become familiar to you. 992px and 600px are known as 'typical breakpoints' for device widths. You will likely see such breakpoints where developers have not embraced more modern layout techniques (which we will discuss in the next chapter). Using the width queries above means that front-end developers can design a page for screens of different widths, ensuring a consistent user experience whether the user accesses the application from a phone or on a regular computer.

Justin Avery (2014) argues that this use of media queries is no longer required as we now have flexbox and grid layouts. Take, for example, Avery's list of typical breakpoints. It contains 24 media queries for various devices, but that list can only grow. It is possible to automate some of the difficulty by using JavaScript, but why not abandon such an approach and use more modern layout techniques to accomplish the same effect with less effort?

While we have primarily looked at querying the width, media queries can detect many other features, which allows for different CSS to be applied depending on the result. Another – and perhaps more useful – way of employing media queries is to implement a separate stylesheet when the user prints the current page (e.g. one that uses absolute units of measurement). Science fiction writer William Hertling (n.d.) has a helpful introduction to printing from the internet and notes that pages can be printed to PDF rather than paper.

Many, perhaps most, of your users will doubtless see your work via a mobile phone, and so it sometimes makes sense to use such devices as the basis for your design. Rather than working towards a finished product which works well on your desktop monitor or laptop screen, you should use empathy and first develop for mobile devices. Such an approach, that of mobile-first or bottom-up development, rather than desktop-first or top-down development, should, in such cases, ease your development process going forward.

CSS calc function
Earlier we explored how CSS measurement units fall into two main groups – absolute and relative – but what happens when you want to mix the two types of unit?

There are rough comparisons between the different units, with all sorts of guides or utilities available online to convert pixels to ems, for example, but they are all approximations, and different devices will, as noted, have different pixel resolutions. How much better would it be if we could use the browser to calculate for us? The `calc` (Mozilla, 2020a) function comes into its own here as we can mix and match measurement units.

I use the `calc` function extensively to ensure that elements within a `div` are correctly positioned and mix percentages with pixels to ensure appropriate positioning.

The `calc` function is particularly useful in situations where the viewport changes. In such cases, the browser does not merely do some simple calculation and store the result as the value to use within the CSS; instead, the `calc` function itself is used as the value for the property. This dynamism is at the heart of the power of the `calc` function. The function can use the four simple operators (add, subtract, multiply and divide) and can even be nested, though browser support for nested `calc` functions is spotty.

> If you have some experience of CSS pre-processors, you might note that the `calc` function is like the math functions of all such pre-processors. `calc` is perhaps another example where evolution in the standard has removed some of the workarounds created by developers – but, in this case, it is far more nuanced, as `calc` is dynamic and reacts to changes in the viewport without having to rely on media queries or clever JavaScript noticing changes in the viewport.

I have been talking primarily about widths of elements as well as font sizes in these sections, but these are not the limits of the `calc` function. Anywhere a `length` (Mozilla, 2019e), `frequency` (Mozilla, 2019b), `angle` (Mozilla, 2019a), `time` (Mozilla, 2019g), `percentage` (Mozilla, 2020h), `number` (Mozilla, 2019f) or `integer` (Mozilla, 2019d) value can be used, it is possible to use the `calc` function. Keep in mind that support can be problematic, though, so it is always worthwhile providing a fallback as, should a browser not support your usage, the `calc` function will be ignored and the previous value will be used instead.

CSS summary
You may perhaps have seen references to CSS3, suggesting that CSS has evolved in a series of stages from 1 through 3. This idea of a step-by-step evolution is false, though, there is no CSS3 standard as such (Mozilla, 2020d), due in part to browser manufacturers dragging their heels while working towards CSS2 from CSS1. It is a continually evolving technology and one that you need to keep abreast of, while continually checking how the browsers you target implement the standard, to ensure you do not waste too much time developing a solution which might not work on your intended browser.

Quite apart from keeping up to date, play with the new techniques, as they will inform your decision making when it comes to creating new or enhancing old applications.

JavaScript

In this section, we will look at the final side of the front-end development triangle, JavaScript.

Initially created by Brendan Eich under the auspices of Netscape in 1995, JavaScript has been 'extended to contexts that range far beyond the initial intent of its designers' (Champeon, 2001).

While under initial development, JavaScript was called Mocha and then LiveScript, but when it was released in Netscape 2.0 it was called JavaScript. Its naming is somewhat controversial. Champeon (2001) writes that it was named LiveScript because it was intended to aid designers with integrating Java applets[9] into web pages, and that its name was changed when Sun and Netscape asserted that it was a complement to HTML and Java. Nicholas Zakas (2005) states that Netscape changed the name in an attempt to cash in on the latest buzzword of the time.

Champeon notes that the changes of name plagued front-end developers for years to come, as the names were confused on mailing lists and Usenet discussions. This confused situation persists to some degree, as even now some call it ECMAScript.[10]

---

9   A Java applet is a program written in Java that can be embedded within an HTML page. They were depreciated in 2017 (when a technology is depreciated, it means that it should no longer be used; for example, while it is still possible to see applets online, the manufacturer discourages their usage).

10 ECMAScript is a specification for a scripting language from the Ecma International standardisation body, whereas JavaScript is the implementation of the specification.

JavaScript can be described as a high-level interpreted programming language (Wikipedia, 2020d). Let's unpack that a little. A 'high-level' language is one that is abstracted from the bare metal of the machine upon which it runs. Rather than using arcane and obscure commands to interact with the registers of the processor, it uses much easier-to-understand, human-friendly language (Wikipedia, 2020b). An 'interpreted' language is one that is executed directly rather than being compiled into machine language (Wikipedia, 2020c). JavaScript relies on an interpreter (sometimes called an engine) to run, and each browser has a slightly different interpreter with slightly different capabilities. The existence of these many different interpreters explains why it used to be so difficult to ensure that JavaScript written with one browser in mind would work in a different browser or even a different version of the same browser, or the identical version on a different architecture (e.g. Windows PC vs Apple Mac). This situation is no longer the case and all evergreen browsers[11] can understand the same JavaScript, although there can be small differences in terms of their speed of operation.

Front-end developers typically use JavaScript to manipulate the DOM and enable richer interfaces in HTML documents. However, interactivity is increasingly becoming the domain of CSS, with enhancements in CSS meaning that JavaScript is now less relevant for such purposes.

JavaScript enables front-end developers to control all the elements within the DOM and change elements and their attributes, as well as to create new elements and remove existing ones. It can also react to events and change the styling of elements within the DOM. This control is so total that more modern JavaScript libraries create a virtual DOM, an abstraction of the HTML DOM detached from the browser's DOM – which itself is an abstraction generated by the browser from the HTML written by the front-end developer. Many modern frameworks, such as Facebook's React, use a

---

11 An evergreen browser is one in which updates are downloaded and installed automatically, ensuring that the user always has the most up-to-date version.

JavaScript-generated virtual DOM to populate the HTML DOM, with a near-empty HTML document merely serving as a base upon which JavaScript builds the page in its entirety.

Despite this power, JavaScript was initially intended to be both a back-end and a front-end language – and, with the recent introduction of Node.js, this is what it has become again.

Node.js is a technology which allows JavaScript to run on the server and it has had a significant impact on the development of front-end JavaScript. This impact has included significant investments in time and effort to improve the development process of JavaScript. The Node Package Manager is now extensively used on the front-end despite originally having been developed to help Node.js developers to discover, share and use JavaScript from other developers working on the back-end. Other outcomes include JavaScript now being recognised as a serious language and improvements in the tools available for JavaScript development. It is primarily a server-side (or back-end) technology, except where it impacts on modern development tooling[12] and toolchains.

> You will see many references to JavaScript libraries and frameworks. There is a difference between these two terms, but it can be a subtle difference at times. I think of libraries as JavaScript tools which allow me to get things done, whereas I see frameworks as guidelines about how things should be done. The distinctions between the two will be explored further below.

I have mentioned JavaScript libraries, and we should look at some of them in greater depth because, even though efforts at standardisation are bearing fruit, the use of certain libraries is

---

12 Many modern JavaScript frameworks use features of the language which are not fully supported in all browsers. There is a wealth of tools within possible JavaScript toolchains and we will look further at some of these later.

still prevalent, if only to support older browsers without more modern features of the language. Perhaps the most popular JavaScript library is jQuery. Different browsers used to have significantly different ways of interacting with the DOM; jQuery simplified DOM tree traversal and manipulation as well as asynchronous JavaScript and XML (AJAX) by providing an abstraction library which – under the hood – used the browser's native ability to make requests to the server.

AJAX

Why was this abstraction (mentioned in the previous paragraph) so important? To explain, we need to look at what AJAX is and why it is important. We have seen that a browser requests an HTML document and renders it onto the screen, and that is generally enough if all you are doing is consuming the information contained in the document (see Figure 2.4).

Figure 2.4 Traditional web usage

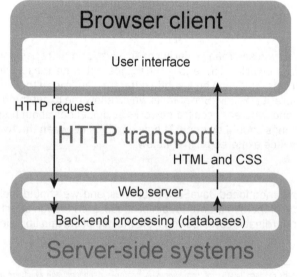

But what happens if you need to interact with the document in some way? We used to have to rely on forms to do this. A user would fill in a form and submit the data back to the server, where it could be processed and stored within a database. If the processing required it, then a further document would be sent to the browser to be displayed, with the whole DOM and CSSOM rendering process occurring at each stage of the process. As you can imagine, for complex interactions, there was a tremendous amount of redundancy with similar content being transported and rendered repeatedly. It also took a painfully long time over slower connections.

Using the browser as nothing more than a dumb terminal seems strange to us, primarily as processing power within clients has increased, but that was how we were limited to doing things online until the development of AJAX.

Jesse James Garrett, who wrote the seminal article which popularised the term 'Ajax', argues that the delay associated with repeated HTTP requests was the primary reason for using AJAX, though he comes at the issue from the direction of user interaction. He said:

> An Ajax application eliminates the start-stop-start-stop nature of interaction on the Web by introducing an intermediary – an Ajax engine – between the user and the server. It seems like adding a layer to the application would make it less responsive, but the opposite is true. (Garrett, 2005)

As you can see from this quote, AJAX allowed a more nuanced approach to interacting with a back-end server. Rather than massive exchanges between the client and the server with a great deal of redundancy, there was an initial hit from loading a slightly larger initial payload, with JavaScript directions and any associated libraries, but then subsequently much smaller transfers of data.

Another interesting point is the use of asynchronous communication, meaning that the client fires off a request and acts upon the result of that request when it is received, rather than waiting for the response (see Figure 2.5). Sometimes this can seem uncomfortable, as we must trust that a result has been sent, but it does improve performance for the user, and the delay often goes unnoticed.

Figure 2.5 AJAX web usage

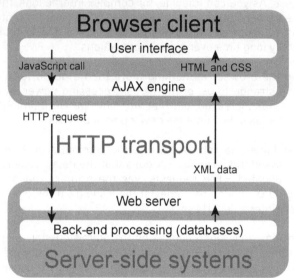

JavaScript libraries
JavaScript libraries are often used to make JavaScript development easier, either by providing a unified way of interacting with the DOM or by manipulating data. Libraries are facing increased competition from frameworks but still offer shortcuts to front-end developers. We will look at some of the most common ones now.

jQuery If you attempted to write an AJAX request in the early days of the technology, using JavaScript without a library, you would have had to code in many conditionals[13] to detect the tools the browsers made available. jQuery solved this problem by abstracting that process away from the developer, and often an AJAX request was made with a one-line function call.

Both Microsoft and Nokia bundle jQuery on their platforms. To an extent this might help to explain its popularity, as the number of corporate developers as well as corporate backing cannot help but boost its usage. Along with backing by some of the most significant players in the market, jQuery enables others to build plugins which address specific needs. It is a library that, at its core, makes use of CSS selectors to interact with the DOM, making use of these selectors on native HTML elements to encourage separation of the JavaScript and HTML by easing the addition of event handlers on elements.

Let me explain this a little more. We can add an event handler to an element by adding a specific attribute to that element using HTML like this:

```
<button id="hello-button"
        onclick="alert('Hello world!')">
    Say Hello
</button>
```

Using jQuery, we could write the same code like this:

```
<button id="hello-button">
    Say Hello
</button>
<script>
    $(() => {
        $("#hello-button")
            .click(() =>
                alert("Hello world!")
            );
    });
</script>
```

---

13 Conditional statements test a condition and do something depending on the result of the test. The most common type is the **if ... else** statement but there are others (Mozilla, 2020g).

The above represents a significant overhead regarding the number of lines of code required to have the same effect, but it does mean there is a separation of concerns (Wikipedia, 2020f). This separation is essential in much the same way as placing CSS in external files is critical; it allows us to reuse the JavaScript in a modular way.

The inline JavaScript in the first example is removed from the HTML and placed within a **script** element; this JavaScript can even be in a separate file elsewhere on the server or a content delivery network. It is a far cleaner approach, with the HTML standing alone as a document but enhanced by the JavaScript once it has been loaded.

It must be pointed out, though, that the jQuery above can now trivially be replaced with JavaScript in more modern browsers, though it is important to check any logs available to you to see whether your audience is using older browsers. Sometimes jQuery will be included as the application depends on one or more plugins which require it, and sometimes there just has not been time to rewrite the application using more modern JavaScript.

This is the equivalent modern JavaScript; it replicates the above jQuery:

```
(() => {
  document
    .querySelector("#hello-button")
    .onclick = () =>
      alert("Hello world!");
})();
```

jQuery also encourages brevity and clarity by using chainable and shorthand functions. More specifically, once we have a handle on one or more elements, we can apply a function to them repeatedly within a chain. Going back to our CSS markup, we could replace the CSS with this jQuery:

```
$(() => {
  $("p").css({
    "color": "#ff0000"
  }).each((index, element) => {
    if($(element)
      .hasClass("emphasis")){
      $(element)
        .css({
          "font-weight": "bold"
        });
    }
    if($(element)
      .attr("id") === "recently-deleted"){
      $(element).css({
        "text-decoration": "linethrough"
      });
    }
  });
});
```

This code illustrates both chaining and brevity. Instead of checking for the **class** attribute, we can use the **hasClass** function, which returns either true or false rather than having to make a specific check on the value of the attribute. The code chains the test for the **emphasis** class and the **id** called **recently-deleted** after setting the colour of all elements to red.

By far jQuery's most useful feature for me as a beginner programmer was the elimination of cross-browser incompatibilities, and, to an extent, this also aided its increased popularity, as it allowed developers to write plugins which would work across all browsers. There is a vast ecosystem of jQuery plugins available which can help you to do all sorts of things, from validating forms to creating image carousels to manipulating tables.

Be wary of relying on jQuery too much, though. As browser manufacturers have worked towards making their JavaScript engines more compliant with developing standards, the need for jQuery has waned. However, that ecosystem of plugins and its ability to play nicely with Vanilla JavaScript[14] means that we will likely see the number of sites bundling jQuery continue to rise for some time yet before it plateaus and goes into a decline. At the time of writing, jQuery is used by 96.4% of all the websites whose JavaScript library is widely known; to put this into context, this is 74.1% of all sites (W3Techs, n.d.).

Other JavaScript libraries   Other JavaScript libraries you are likely to come across are Bootstrap, Underscore.js, MooTools, Lodash and Modernizr. At the time of writing, these are the most popular libraries, but these statistics are bound to change over time. The sheer momentum behind these libraries, however, means that they will likely still be in play for some time to come.

> The inclusion of Bootstrap in this list is perhaps odd in that Bootstrap includes several jQuery plugins and so usually requires jQuery as well – though there are conversions of Bootstrap to JavaScript frameworks, such as Angular, React and Vue (which are explored further below).

These other JavaScript libraries all, to some degree or another, seek to address cross-browser incompatibilities. Modernizr works to achieve this by detecting browser features (Modernizr, n.d.) and Underscore.js provides over a hundred functions which are generally unsupported by older browsers (Underscore, 2018). Despite its utility, Underscore.js seems to be being superseded somewhat by Lodash at present as, while they offer similar functionality, Lodash provides a much more consistent API (application programming interface) while also providing additional functions. It may well be that you will come across both while looking at older code. If so, I would suggest that you investigate the removal of one or the other to reduce the dependencies in the application.

---

14 Vanilla JavaScript, or VanillaJS, is a term often used to remind developers that they don't always need to use a framework or library. Many times using the language itself will suffice.

I use (and envisage continuing to use) any number of libraries each day in my development practice, but often these are more niche libraries, such as D3 (Bostock, 2017) for creating interactive visualisations, Moment.js to help with using dates and times in JavaScript, and p5.js for teaching programming concepts to primary school students. Numeral.js is also useful and acts in a similar way to Moment.js, but for numbers rather than dates and times.

It is crucial to keep abreast of new libraries and to continue learning to maintain your relevance as a front-end developer and improve your employment prospects.

JavaScript frameworks

There are many JavaScript frameworks, and I have used most, if not all, of them. I have also been bitten by choosing the wrong one.

A framework is distinguished from a library in that a framework defines the entire application design, whereas a library offers functions to be called by code. Another way of looking at the difference is in terms of control; we developers call the functions of a library, whereas a framework provides the skeleton which we need to flesh out with code, sometimes from a library.

At the time of writing, there are three significant frameworks, and they continually jockey for pole position (Biton, 2018). These are React, Angular and Vue, and we will briefly look at each. It is a matter of choice which one you want to invest your time in learning, but I will make some suggestions. To an extent, spending time familiarising yourself with all of them is worthwhile as it will broaden your appeal to potential employers; however, there is a growing appreciation that knowing one in greater depth will not hurt, as the concepts learnt are transferable.

Before you begin, however, you should always decide whether a framework is required or whether Vanilla JavaScript would suffice. ES6,[15] sometimes also known as ECMAScript 2015, has seen considerable improvements in the language, and it is now more elegant to read and write as well as being a thorough delight to use as it seems to me to be so much more expressive. A more prolonged examination of the changes in JavaScript is beyond the scope of this book. However, if you find yourself in the unfortunate position of needing to support Internet Explorer 11, be aware that there are tools available, such as Babel, which will transform your modern code into code suitable for older browsers.

React   There is some discussion about whether React can be called a framework, with many thinking of it more as a library (Petrosyan, 2018). Indeed, it is primarily used as the 'view' in a model–view–controller (MVC) application.[16] React bridges the distinction between a framework and a library while sharing the component-based architecture of many other frameworks, so I consider it valid to discuss it in this section rather than the section concerned with JavaScript libraries.

React was initially developed under the auspices of Facebook and is grounded in a similar PHP-based technology also developed by Facebook.

React makes use of a virtual DOM to make selected changes to the HTML DOM by calculating the differences between the in-memory representation of the HTML DOM and the actual representation of the document. Using the virtual DOM means that subtle changes are made without the whole page reloading. This might seem memory-intensive until one appreciates the increasing resources available to client applications in browsers, regardless of the architecture on which the browser resides.

---

15 The sixth edition of ECMAScript was a significant update to JavaScript. It is widely used and compatible with all evergreen browsers (browsers that are automatically upgraded to the latest version).

16 An application design model composed of three interconnected parts: the model (data), the view (user interface) and the controller (processes that handle input).

One crucial thing about React is its use of JavaScript XML (JSX), which is an extension of JavaScript syntax and allows developers to write HTML-like syntax within JavaScript rather than relying upon the browser's API methods to create elements. The following represents a simple 'Hello World' application in React:

```
class HelloWorld extends React.Component {
  render() {
    return (
      <p>Hello World</p>
    );
  }
}


ReactDOM.render(
  <HelloWorld/>,
  document.querySelector('#app')
);
```

JSX can leave some feeling uncomfortable as it mixes HTML with JavaScript. An alternative is to use the methods built into React to create an HTML element rather than using React to parse JSX. The result can then be used to create HTML elements, like this:

```
class HelloWorld extends React.Component {
  render() {
    return React.createElement(
      "p",
      null,
      "Hello World!"
    )
  }
}


ReactDOM.render(
  <HelloWorld/>,
  document.querySelector('#app')
);
```

React can be used in conjunction with another library to manage the state of an application. One such library is Redux. This reliance on external libraries can be problematic for those coming from an MVC background, though, as the concept is slightly different in the world of React and Redux. Rather than models, views and controllers, React and Redux have actions, reducers, stores and components. There is an interesting analogy on the blog *Hackernoon* which goes into greater detail (Levkovsky, 2017).

Angular   There are now two distinct flavours of Angular. Both are being used extensively in production environments, with later versions becoming more prevalent over time as people update their legacy systems.

AngularJS   The original Angular is often called AngularJS or Angular 1. It was developed in 2009 by Miško Hevery (n.d.) and Adam Abrons (Austin, 2014) and was written in JavaScript. To an extent, it kicked off the development of many other frameworks. It was revolutionary in that it acknowledged that HTML is primarily for the display of static documents and that previous efforts at making it dynamic had, by and large, failed. It was initially developed to offer developers the ability to interact with both the front- and the back-end of applications. However, after Hevery made a wager that he could refactor a 17,000-line application using his framework (then called GetAngular) in a fortnight, it became the darling of Google. He took three weeks to refactor the application and replaced the 17,000 lines with 1,500.

Due to its age and it being superseded by current versions of Angular, it would perhaps not be appropriate for a new front-end developer to spend too much time familiarising themselves with AngularJS, unless they have been tasked with maintaining a legacy system. A glance at the documentation should suffice.

Angular   Rather than being written in 100% JavaScript as AngularJS was, Angular (also known as Angular 2+ or Angular v2 and beyond) is a complete rewrite using Microsoft's TypeScript.

TypeScript is a superset of JavaScript and offers optional static typing despite the fact that it can be transpiled to conformant JavaScript. JavaScript's lack of static typing is one of the significant complaints aimed at it. TypeScript's static typing has eased JavaScript's adoption within Enterprise, where such typing is prevalent in languages such as C#.

Most, if not all, of the other JavaScript frameworks can be prototyped quickly on platforms such as JSFiddle,[17] but Angular requires transpilation, which is beyond the capabilities of that platform. There are various platforms which facilitate Angular development, but even the most straightforward programs often require a significant overhead (in terms of the tools required) for the associated infrastructure to transpile the TypeScript.

Angular is undoubtedly popular in the realm of Enterprise, but this is continuously changing, with React taking a significant chunk of market share in 2018 (Elliott, 2017). Angular's popularity in part stems from its age, as it was the first framework to be released and so many developers are used to working with it. With its use of TypeScript, it is also easy to transition to from other statically typed languages, such as Microsoft's C#. Proponents of Angular point out that it saves time, is easy to learn, has excellent data-binding, offers a declarative expression of the user interface (UI) and is free (Thinkwik, 2017). However, both Angular and React are under threat by the next framework we will examine.

Vue Also known as Vue.js, this is most often written in ES6, and there are syntax styles associated with it. Like Angular, it has roots in Google, but it came about from its primary developer, Evan You, who said:

---

17 JSFiddle is a popular online integrated development environment that allows developers to quickly prototype and test HTML, CSS and JavaScript within the browser.

I figured, what if I could just extract the part that I really liked about Angular and build something really lightweight without all the extra concepts involved? (Cromwell, 2017)

Rather than following MVC architecture, Vue uses a model–view–viewmodel (MVVM)[18] architecture. The distinctions between these architectures are convoluted and confused. It might be worthwhile playing with each and then deciding how you would prefer your systems to be architected. Suffice it to say that the controller is replaced with a viewmodel.

Rather than using a separate language like JSX, Vue can use template HTML elements (Mozilla, 2020i), and it is designed to be incrementally adoptable with there being a strong suggestion that developers can replace jQuery with Vue (Drasner, 2018). While it is possible to embed Vue within an application, perhaps sourced from a content delivery network, and start using it immediately, a developer can also take advantage of modern toolchains like that used by Angular. This flexibility means that Vue has attracted an enormous audience, as you can start coding when there is no internet connection. Its minified size (86KB) is comparable to modern jQuery (87KB), and it has so much more to offer, though it is possible to use both on the same page.

Just like React, Vue utilises a virtual DOM. It also has a similar approach to components to both Angular and React. It borrows extensively from both frameworks (H & V, n.d.) and is better for appropriating and implementing similar strategies. This derivation of strategy and technique might also aid its adoption by developers used to one of the other popular frameworks: should you be feeling limited by your current framework, the learning curve associated with switching to Vue is likely to be less steep than that of moving between Angular and React (Value Coders, 2018).

---

18 The MVC format is specifically designed to create a separation of concerns *between* the model and view, while the MVVM format (which uses data-binding) is designed specifically to allow the view and model to communicate directly with each other.

The Vue website provides a comprehensive comparison of Vue with other frameworks (George, 2018).

Other frameworks   Along with the big three JavaScript frameworks, there are many more, such as Ember (Tilde Inc., 2018), Knockout (Sanderson, n.d.), Polymer (Polymer Project, 2018) and Riot (RIOT, 2018). Their number is continually growing, so it is wise to keep an eye on resources such as ThoughtWorks' Technology Radar (ThoughtWorks, 2018).

I think that one of the reasons we have so many frameworks is down to front-end developers. It used to be that to be able to call oneself a developer one had to have written at least one content management system (Palas, 2017). Perhaps now we are entering a world where to call yourself a proper developer you need to have written your own, distinct, framework or library?

Many such frameworks are likely to be superseded, some sooner rather than later. The toolchain involved in building even the smallest single-page application is enormous and can be confusing, and it is gradually being made redundant by developments within JavaScript itself. Whereas once we needed module bundlers (tools which take JavaScript and any dependencies the code might have, such as libraries used, and bundle them all into a single file) and module loaders (libraries for loading, interpreting and executing JavaScript modules) in the form of tools such as Webpack and Browserfy, we are now in a period where we have native modules (though it is likely that we will need to continue using module bundlers for at least a few more years, as native modules are still not fully supported in all major browsers – or we may at least need to use both methods).

MODULES

What are modules, I hear you say? Let me explain. In modular programming, we use a software design technique which separates the functionality of a program into distinct modules. So, we could have a module dedicated to handling dates and times (e.g. Moment.js) and another dedicated to dealing with charts (e.g. D3), which could, in turn, be split into modules dealing with different types of chart. So, an application could be made up of any number of files, and the order of their loading could be an issue; a jQuery plugin needs to be aware of jQuery before it can act upon the page, for instance.

Browsers used to be quite bad at dealing with these situations, but that is less and less the case. However, what does all this mean to us front-end developers? It means that we can make use of distinct modules in native JavaScript without having to be overly concerned with a toolchain to transpile and bundle our code.

Native modules seem to be another of those situations where the evolving technology has taken over from workarounds. This progression is something to be welcomed, and I guess that it was only through noticing the pain-points associated with using JavaScript to manipulate animation and conflicting module definitions that the industry created or adapted existing standards.

JAVASCRIPT TOOLCHAIN

I have mentioned the term 'toolchain' already, but what does it mean? We have looked at how JavaScript is loaded into the browser, but the generation of that JavaScript can, depending on requirements, involve using many libraries or frameworks, and bundling them all together can be problematic. This is where a toolchain comes in handy.

There are three main components in a JavaScript toolchain:

- package manager;
- bundler;
- compiler.

Package manager

You will find throughout your career that someone somewhere has already accomplished many of the things you are trying to do, and often they have made their code available to others in a library. You can 'borrow' their work using a package manager.

There are two primary package managers you will likely see: Node Package Manager and Facebook's YARN. Both of these package managers use a manifest file to keep track of the libraries and packages you are using as well as their versions. They also identify any dependencies the packages require and install them. Finally, they should generate a lock file which contains all the information needed to reproduce the full dependency source tree[19] – this means that the whole dependency source tree can be regenerated later. This mechanism is particularly valuable when it comes to saving your work in a version control system (covered in the next section), as the amount of code transferred can be limited to only your work.

---

19 A dependency source tree lists all the packages and their version, along with each package's dependencies, so that they can be downloaded again later.

Bundler

Bundlers combine and compress many different JavaScript files into one single file and thus reduce the number of downloads required by the browser (although modern browsers can now download multiple files at once). We touched on bundles when we examined frameworks. A standard module system was introduced in 2015 as part of ES6, but before that there were several different ways of making JavaScript modules. Despite my preference for using native modules without a bundler, support for earlier browsers and the other optimisations offered by bundlers mean that they are likely to be required in at least the short to medium term.

The other tools provided by bundlers include minimising the size of the resultant code as well as a facility for using plugins to transpile SCSS[20] into CSS, for example. There are many different bundlers, so it is worth doing some research to find one that will accomplish what you require.

Compiler

Often called by the bundler, the compiler will allow you to write modern JavaScript with the understanding that the resultant code will work in older browsers. By far the most popular compiler at the time of writing is Babel.

JavaScript summary

JavaScript has been called 'the world's most misunderstood programming language' (Crockford, 2001) because, underneath its simplicity, there is a great deal of power. It is also an evolving language and one with which you will

---

20 SCSS is a more modern type of Syntactically Awesome Style Sheets, which is a dialect of CSS.

doubtless become familiar if you choose to become a front-end developer. However, I would advise you to spend some time becoming familiar with it even if you do not decide to become a front-end developer. I use it regularly in my non-work-related life when writing apps and scripts to run in Google Sheets to calculate my day-to-day finances, for example. The wealth of learning resources can be overwhelming, but I would suggest starting with MDN Web Docs (https://developer.mozilla.org).

OTHER TOOLS

Along with our front-end development triangle, there are many other tools with which you should be at least slightly familiar. Let's look at some of them.

Version control system

When you start working in development, you may not appreciate the need for a version control system (VCS), but it will probably not be long before you make an unrecoverable mistake or your local machine suffers some form of failure, leaving all your work lost to the aether. This is where a VCS is worth its weight in gold! A VCS tracks your changes to code and provides you with control over them.

A VCS is also of paramount importance when working within a team as it allows changes made by different developers to be merged into a cohesive whole, while mitigating the chance of code being lost.

By far the most popular VCS is Git. While initially it can seem daunting, you can get by with a small number of commands. With many graphical UIs now being available (such as Atlassian's Sourcetree (Atlassian, 2018) and GitHub's own GitHub Desktop (GitHub, 2018)), there is a much lower barrier to using Git.

> There are other VCS options, but another reason for choosing Git is that pointing people to your GitHub[21] profile is an excellent way of demonstrating your abilities.
>
> As well as maintaining your own set of GitHub repositories (or 'repos' – locations where all the files associated with a project are stored), contributing to other projects on GitHub is a fantastic way of raising your profile as a developer – and there is nothing quite so exciting as having a pull request accepted by a high-profile repo.[22]

A wealth of free and paid resources are available for you to access when it comes to learning Git. Git allows users to track changes to files across different users and merge those changes into a final file. It is a distributed VCS, so many users can work on the same project at the same time, with all those changes being unified into a single, master branch. Often these merges take place in a web-based hosting service, such as GitHub, although there are many other services available, such as Bitbucket, SourceForge and GitLab, to name just three.

Editor and integrated development environment

The choice of editor and integrated development environment (IDE) is another area where you will find many conflicting opinions – sometimes from the same person over time. This is where you will spend much of your time as a front-end developer, so it is well worth testing the options. There used to be significant differences between editors and IDEs, but some editors have plugins which give them IDE-like capabilities.

---

21 GitHub provides external hosting for Git repositories (repos). This means that once your code has been committed to a repo and the commit has been pushed to GitHub, it can be retrieved on another device and development can be continued. It is also an excellent mechanism for backing up your work.

22 A pull request is made when you want to make changes to a Git repo. The owner of the repo can commit the pull request to the relevant branch (a working copy of the code).

Editors

Typically, an editor is merely a tool which allows you to edit text. Not all editors are equal – it might be appropriate to suggest that Microsoft Word is an editor, but it is unsuited to some tasks, in much the same way that Microsoft's Notepad is unsuited to writing a dissertation, for instance.

This is not to say that you cannot write code in Microsoft Word (Paulb, 2012) – there is a Japanese gentleman who uses Microsoft Excel to create stunning art (Pinar, 2017), after all – but it would perhaps be best to use an editor better suited to the task.

It is common to find that developers use more than one editor during their work. This profligate use of editors is because each has its strengths and weaknesses.

During my day, I will often have Sublime Text (Sublime HQ Pty Ltd, 2018) and Brackets.io (Adobe, 2018) open at the same time. I use Brackets.io because of its useful Live Preview (Adobe, 2017), which helps with the rapid prototyping of concepts that I am working on, and Sublime Text because of its sheer sophistication.

I have a favourite editor in Boxer (Hamel, 2018b), though. I install it on every machine I use because of its ability to wrangle text and because I am familiar with it and its powerful macro capability (Hamel, 2018a).

Integrated development environments

An IDE includes an editor, but only as part of a more comprehensive suite of tools required to write, test and deploy projects. The other tools will likely include build automation (meaning you can configure your IDE to transpile SCSS for you) and a debugger, which you should be able to attach to an instance of a browser. This attachment to a browser instance means that code you change should be reflected in the browser without having to go through the process of being deployed to a server.

While I would encourage you to spread your affections regarding your use of editors, being extravagant in your use of IDEs is less than ideal. There are IDEs which have a particular focus on a technology stack, such as Visual Studio, which is used to develop .NET languages; PHPStorm (developed by JetBrains), which is used to develop with PHP; and Eclipse, which is used for Java development. However, most IDEs can be made to work with a range of languages.

Visual Studio is seeking to widen its reach, especially with the introduction of the free Community edition (Wikipedia, 2020e) in 2014. With the wealth of plugins available, the Visual Studio Code editor is approaching an IDE in terms of its facilities.

Choosing editors and integrated development environments

There are things you should be aware of when choosing editors and IDEs. Of course, you might find that some editors and IDEs are suited to different aspects of your work; you might develop a preference for a particular editor for developing CSS, another for HTML and a third for JavaScript. This is perfectly acceptable, and it might even be the case that an editor or IDE you initially disregarded is improved in a newer release, tempting you to try it again.

Typography   While we are usually interested in the typeface we display to our users, we also likely have preferences when it comes to the appearance of our code. Though this preference is likely to be assuaged by an understanding that the typeface is of less importance than the code we are writing, is it essential to use a typeface which aids the parsing of your code. Using a non-fixed-width typeface is possible and some developers say that it aids their comprehension of the code, although there are arguments against it – for example, in code it is important for each individual character to be correct, and fixed-width typefaces enable developers to find typos quickly.

My preference is for Dank Mono (Plückthun, 2018), designed by Phil Plückthun. The primary reason I like it so much is aesthetic more than anything. When a test for equality occurs in JavaScript, we use three equals signs (===), and when Dank Mono is used to do this, it replaces the three equals signs with three horizontal lines of the same width as the three individual characters. Arrow functions (=>) also look much more like arrows and the non-equality operator looks like a gate.

These seem like very minor reasons for spending my hard-earned money on something which no one else will notice, but such moments of delight are what we are trying to engender in our audience. It seems like the worst kind of masochism to avoid producing the same moments of happiness for ourselves.

Themes   Closely linked to the issue of typefaces are themes. Most editors and IDEs allow their users to alter at least the colour scheme of their interface, and some enable many more configurable options. You will spend so much time looking at the code you're working on that you need a theme which will not strain your eyes, especially in different external lighting conditions.

There is significant debate about themes so I would suggest downloading and installing some (if your choice of editor/ IDE allows theming) and trying them out. Sometimes merely changing the theme is enough to improve your workflow, as it prevents the tool from becoming stale and allows more moments of delight as you notice subtle enhancements.

THE MOST IMPORTANT TOOL

I have saved the most critical tool until last: you.

All front-end developers I know have the qualities in this section to some degree or another. That is not to say that they are not shared by other types of developer, but they are particularly crucial for those developers who are responsible for creating the interface between the rest of the team and the users of the system that is being developed.

Empathy

Empathy is the ability to put yourself into the shoes of someone else. In front-end development it allows the practitioner to have some idea of the state of mind of someone visiting a web application or website for the very first time, and of those who have perhaps visited many times before but who have been confronted with a change in the interface. We do not always know who our users are, except in certain circumstances: they could be from any walk of life and have different abilities and experiences. While we cannot necessarily know all or any of our users, we can imagine them and their circumstances and seek to provide an enjoyable, or at least stress-free, experience. In the case of changes to an interface, this needs to be handled sensitively as not everyone is comfortable with change. Trying to understand what users might be thinking and feeling will inform your design and development decisions in such an instance.

At the beginning of my previous career as a psychiatric nurse, one of my earliest lectures was on the difference between sympathy and empathy. Sympathy is an older term than empathy, but generally it suggests that someone feels pity for another, and pity is not helpful. Sympathy is an *emotion* whereas empathy is an *ability*, and it is an ability which can constantly be developed to empower your work as a front-end developer.

Listening and understanding

Listening is essential for a front-end developer and understanding what you are listening to even more so. There may be all sorts of reasons why someone has reached their own beliefs and conclusions, and it is only through listening and attempting to see things from their perspective that you can hope to achieve an understanding of why they think the way they do.

This is not to say that you should expend significant effort trying to explore why a client might want a colour range to contain a set of colours in a nonsensical order, or whether a quartile should be displayed as five quantiles. Sometimes the client is right, even if they are not really, and so ensuring they are satisfied with the final product of your efforts, despite missing opportunities that are obvious to you, is important. Knowing when to bow out gracefully is sometimes the best that one can hope for, but please do be aware of your ethical responsibility too (more on this in the next chapter).

As well as trying to understand the person you are listening to, it is worth spending some time trying to understand yourself. Dedicating as much, if not more, attention to your own biases as you spend examining others will help you to develop an open mind and self-acceptance.

A further aspect of understanding is an appreciation of the setting of your users. We sometimes imagine our users in a similar environment to ourselves. We imagine them sitting in comfortable chairs, in front of a monitor or two, and warm, dry and well fed and watered. What, then, would we think of someone interacting with our work while sitting on public transport, perhaps surrounded by others while hungry and thirsty, and pressured in terms of time and attention? I mentioned above that empathy is the ability to wear the shoes of others, but might it not be better to not only wear those shoes but also walk the same streets?

Communication

You will doubtless be involved in asking many questions in your career. There are several facets to this, but here we are looking at communication in the context of empathy.

Sometimes just asking a client or user how they think things should be done will help you to reach a joint conclusion. They might have experience of a particularly enjoyable UI that they want to use again or replicate. Sometimes such an interface will be impracticable, but even so, it is still worth discovering what it is and why they were so engaged with it. It might be that you will have to explain why it is inappropriate in this context or is impracticable. Alternatively, you might agree with them that it is the better approach and so change the solution to include it. It is brilliant to learn from our clients, and this possibility should be embraced rather than rejected out of misplaced pride – you should spend your whole career learning!

If you are unable to communicate with your clients, you will have to rely upon having an empathetic understanding of them and take a best guess. However, you will need to be able to justify your decisions.

If you find yourself dealing with any communication issues – for instance, with an abrasive or aggressive client – you should endeavour to remain calm, not argue, and try to listen and understand what is behind the aggression. If you are unable to reach a solution, the communication should be ended as safely and as amicably as possible.

Curiosity

As a front-end developer you need to be curious – curious about the product you will be working on so that you can understand why your users will be using it, as well as curious about the work your colleagues will be doing, as that will inform your own. You will also likely need to be curious about what the end-user will be expecting to see on the screen, before, during and after each interaction.

You will need to be curious more widely too, to keep abreast of the latest developments in your field, and this is no simple matter. Whereas other professions, such as nursing, expect you to carry out post-registration education and practice, this is not the case within front-end development – or, for that matter, other areas of development. Organisations such as BCS, The Chartered Institute for IT aim to remedy this situation somewhat.

In the world of IT, anyone can decide that they are now a practitioner – with no formal requirements for training or continued professional development. While it is arguable that nurses should be demonstrably competent because they are responsible for the care of others, there are roles within IT which share comparable responsibilities (such as when developers work with medical software) but without the equivalent prerequisites or scrutiny.

I feel somewhat uncomfortable with this lack of obligation for IT practitioners to engage in any continued professional development. That is why I am a member of BCS and I would encourage you to join as well – not because it is a requirement for membership of the profession, but because it demonstrates an intention to be responsible for your practice.

A news aggregator such as Feedly can be useful to keep an eye on the developments within your field, but there are many, many other resources available. Email newsletters and podcasts, as well as conferences and meetups,[23] can be

---

23 A meetup is way for predominantly online communities to meet in real life. These online communities are varied and not limited to technology – the endeavour started as a result of Scott Heiferman wanting to meet his New York neighbours after the 9/11 attacks.

especially helpful, so it is worth reaching out to your fellow local developers and seeing what is available in your area.

It may be difficult to scrutinise the competence of IT professionals properly, especially in front-end development, because of the stratification of this role: how, for instance, would one expect to assess the abilities of a developer who specialises in CSS and pre- and post-processors, alongside a developer who specialises in the React framework? Both developers will likely carry out much the same work but will have specialist knowledge in their realms.

Resilience

A 2018 survey carried out by Blind (Cimpanu, 2018) revealed that 57% of tech workers suffer from some form of 'burnout'. Burnout is characterised as exhaustion and is caused by stress, most often the stress of not being able to work in a way in which you are comfortable.

Aside from financial security, why is working important? Occupational therapists and others will tell you that work is a vital part of our identity, despite most people wishing for a life of leisure. Those in meaningful employment are generally healthier and live longer, more fulfilled lives. You need to work, not just to put a roof over your head but to enjoy a longer life, so please do not let your employment harm your health by allowing stress to overwhelm you. If you are unhappy, look at changing employer or even career.

Developing a healthy work–life balance is of paramount importance. You will likely spend decades working, but you won't be working every hour of every day of those decades, so ensuring that your interests, family, and social and leisure activities receive the attention they deserve will all improve your resilience.

AVOIDING IMPOSTER SYNDROME

Throughout this book, I am conscious that I have touched upon many technologies (as well as all sorts of other subjects), and I will continue doing so for the rest of it, but note that you are not expected to know everything! I am by no means an expert, but I am interested in learning and cannot think of a time when I might feel that I have learnt enough. I dare say you are similar, or else why would you be reading this book?

This curiosity and subsequent acknowledgement that we do not know everything is perhaps why developers sometimes suffer from 'imposter syndrome'. Imposter syndrome is a psychological pattern in which an individual doubts their accomplishments and feels a persistent fear that they will be exposed as a fraud.

Imposter syndrome is rife in the world of IT. Perhaps the best advice I have seen for overcoming it comes from Dr Sue Black via Girl's Guide to Project Management (Harrin, 2017) and involves first acknowledging your feelings to yourself and others – you will doubtless find that your colleagues share your anxieties to some degree. I suggest that you do some research of your own and recognise the symptoms of imposter syndrome – and work up some strategies for how to combat it when (not if) you feel it.

It is also important to acknowledge that sometimes imposter syndrome prompts you to learn more, which is no bad thing in itself, but it can be overwhelming and damaging.

SUMMARY

In this chapter we have looked at the most critical tools for front-end developers and ended by pointing out that by far the most important tool has absolutely nothing to do with technology. While an understanding of technology is undoubtedly essential, knowing how to do something is less important than understanding why you want to do it. I mentioned delight in the preface to this book, and not the least part of that delight is that the field is continually changing and you will be continuously challenged not only by advances in techniques but also by trends. Please do continue to learn and hone your skills but never neglect empathy in particular – especially for yourself. Be gentle with yourself.

3   METHODS AND TECHNIQUES

In the previous chapter, we looked at the main tools used by front-end developers every day in their practice. Along with the front-end development triangle of HTML, CSS and JavaScript, there are methods and techniques which a front-end developer will likely need to be aware of, and we will look at some of those in this chapter.

AGILE

There are many approaches to software development and management, including the Waterfall and Spiral methodologies, but by far the most popular at present is Agile. In fact, Agile came about when a group of individuals were brainstorming alternatives to traditional methodologies such as Waterfall and Spiral. This group met in early 2001 and developed the Agile Manifesto (https://agilemanifesto.org), which has at its heart four values that we will look at in the subsections below.

According to Lexico, Agile is defined as:

> Relating to or denoting a method of project management, used especially for software development, that is characterized by the division of tasks into short phases of work and frequent reassessment and adaptation of plans.
>
> [A]gile methods replace high-level design with frequent redesign. (Oxford University Press, n.d.)

What does that mean in practice, though?

When we undertake a development task, we can become overwhelmed by the sheer amount of work which is scheduled. There will be the underlying infrastructure (often server-side, though more frequently serverless[1]) to provision. There will be the logic associated with that infrastructure and any associated technologies required.

Somewhere there should be someone with an understanding of the overall architecture of the project, and that architect will have their own biases related to the programming language and datastore – either SQL or NoSQL (more on these later in this chapter) – which should be employed. There might be a designer with a vision for how the application should look, and there will hopefully be at least one front-end developer tasked with making sure that the designer's vision can interact appropriately with everything below the application in the stack of technologies.

All this can, and often does, lead to confusion. A little like the famed terror which confronts an artist faced with a blank canvas (Landi, 2014), the fear, uncertainty and dread associated with starting a new project can seem overwhelming. This is the situation Agile hopes to address.

The second part of the quote above seems the most appropriate for the start of the development process. Instead of spending an age planning out every part of the final application, the team can concentrate on producing a minimal viable product.

The minimal viable product (MVP) is a concept from Lean Startup[2] (Wikipedia, 2020g) and classically means creating something basic to gain an idea of the interest

---

1   Serverless infrastructure does not imply an absence of servers, but instead means that the servers are managed by a provider who manages the resources required by the server.

2   Lean Startup is a way of developing products in an iterative way. It involves investigating and experimenting with solutions and subsequently rigorously testing those solutions in order to inform the development of the next iteration of the solution.

associated with a new product. Some or all of the business logic of an MVP may be mocked up or even reliant upon human interaction,[3] and it is most suitably used to gauge the interest of users, effectively meaning that the initial offering may only represent a 'vision' of the final product rather than a working prototype. 'MVP' can be used to describe the first iteration of an application within the Agile methodology, but this is not strictly an appropriate use of the phrase.

Within an Agile methodology, an application is initially produced and then undergoes multiple iterations until it is deemed acceptable. While this might also be the case for more traditional methodologies, such as Waterfall, there is within those methodologies an understanding that there is flow towards a finished product, whereas Agile embraces the concept of an ever-improving solution rather than working through a defined process; Agile is far looser in its approach.

As noted earlier, Agile came about partly because of frustration with the over-regulation imposed by so-called heavyweight methodologies. Agile is classified as lightweight and has the following four values.

Individuals and interactions over processes and tools

The Waterfall methodology dictates the process to be followed while developing software (gather requirements for the software, design the software, implement the software, verify the suitability of the software and maintain the software). In contrast, Agile suggests that it is the interaction of skilled and competent developers working together that makes development work. While tools and processes can be used,

---

3   Answers to queries might be found by taking a 'best guess' approach, or the queries might even be answered by human agents, rather than developing a back-end infrastructure.

they should only be used while they are making things easy and effective for the developers.

Working software over comprehensive documentation

The requirements-gathering part of the Waterfall process detailed above, along with the writing of test cases, layouts, specifications and a list of features, can amount to a significant amount of documentation. This documentation may well be out of date by the time the software has been completed, and the users might never use some features.

Agile prefers working software over documentation. This software can then be released to users who, in turn, provide feedback on what extra features or improvements they require. This leads to a far quicker and much more iterative approach to development.

Customer collaboration over contract negotiation

Alongside a reduction in documentation, the iterative process of Agile means that customer collaboration is vital. Rather than meeting with customers at the beginning and end of the project, as in the Waterfall methodology, Agile encourages constant collaboration, with feedback being sought immediately to inform development – hopefully leading to greater customer satisfaction.

Responding to change over following a plan

Change can be challenging in all walks of life. The Waterfall methodology minimised its impact by making detailed plans and methodologies mandatory and strictly adhered to those plans and methodologies. Agile, alternatively, embraces the concept that the only thing that is constant is change,[4] and this allows the developers to embrace change and respond to altered requirements during the process of software

---

4 A concept whose first known iteration came from Heraclitus in about 500BC.

development. In this way, change is seen less as a problem and rather as an opportunity.

Agile has at its heart the concept of the sprint, which is a duration of time (most often a week or fortnight) used by a Scrum team (a team of people of different specialisations). The sprint should accomplish a set of stories. It ends after a specified period, and any stories left over are either carried forward to the next sprint or moved into the backlog (which is a collection of stories held in reserve, should all stories be completed within the sprint).

> It must be noted that Scrum is one Agile methodology and that there are others. Kanban is one and is similar to Scrum, but Kanban does not prescribe a particular workflow, nor does it have defined roles as Scrum does, such as Scrum master, product owner and team member. It also places a far greater emphasis on system thinking rather than being team-centric. For a more detailed exploration of the differences, see LeanKit (2018).

Stories are discrete units of work, such as implementing an area of new functionality within an application. They are allocated story points, which indicate their complexity, rather than the length of time they should take to complete. As you can probably imagine, a task which one developer might see as complex, another will find easier, depending on their level of experience or ability, so the story points are decided collaboratively. Deciding whether a story can be marked as completed can be problematic, with some teams requiring acceptance testing[5] by a user and others accepting the decision of either another developer or a dedicated quality assurance (QA) tester.

---

5 Acceptance testing evaluates whether the system is compliant with the requirements of the business and is carried out before the system is released for delivery to the end users. It is most often carried out by the product owner.

In my current team – despite the emphasis on story points representing complexity – we assign two story points to a day, so a typical fortnight-long sprint will see a developer being assigned 20 story points' worth of work. This assignment is slightly against the principles of Scrum, in that it uses story points to represent time rather than complexity – but it must be noted that 'a Story Point is a relative unit of measure, decided upon and used by individual Scrum teams, to provide relative estimates of effort for completing requirements' (Davidson, 2014).

Progress on Agile projects is discussed, briefly, in a daily stand-up (also known as the 'morning rollcall' or 'daily scrum') where each member details their progress and plans for the coming day. Stand-ups can also be used to raise issues and garner ideas from other members. These issues might take the form of impediments or blockers (Carlton, 2016). Alternatively, a developer might be confronted by an issue which is beyond their capabilities but is not beyond those of other members of the team. In such cases, the stand-up enables help to be offered as soon as possible. The number of points completed in a sprint serves as a measure of the Scrum team's velocity and will influence the number of story points allocated to the Scrum for the next sprint.

I suggest that you spend some time reading and learning more about Agile. However, suffice to say that, like many revolutionary approaches, it has in many cases become just as rigid as the methodologies it replaced, in my opinion. Methodology can suffocate a developer if imposed too strictly.

TECHNIQUES

Many of the techniques examined in this section will be employed on many of the websites you interact with each day. We interact with those sites using a browser, and browsers have a wealth of tools for front-end developers built-in.

> You should become familiar with inspecting the elements of a web page, even if you do not pursue a career as a front-end developer. It is almost like going behind the curtain in Oz to discover that all the exciting things you can see are just made up of words.
>
> Learning about the developer tools, and likewise teaching them to someone, is empowering. They allow us to understand what is going on behind the scenes and alter it, if only in the local context. Additionally, the ability to use a browser's JavaScript interpreter from the developer console[6] means that you can solve maths problems without having to use a calculator.

Once you get into the habit of thinking about the things that confront you in a browser in an investigative way, by interrogating them using the developer tools, many mysteries will be made manifest. You will gain valuable insights into how other front-end developers have achieved their aims.

Forms

A web application is of very little use without some input from the user. Imagine your day-to-day interactions on the internet – do you find yourself entering information into forms? Even if it is only your name and email address to subscribe to an email newsletter, you will be using a form. We can garner

---

6   MDN Web Docs has an excellent article on the developer console and the other tools available within a browser (Mozilla, 2020j).

information from our users without forms, but, in terms of gathering rich and detailed information from them, forms are beyond compare.

> HTML 2 introduced the **form** element. Early internet forms required the user to either download them, fill them in and then email them back or print them, fill them in and post them to the webmaster (Editorial Team, 2016). Thankfully we are much more nuanced these days, and nearly every interaction with officialdom can be carried out online.

At their most basic, and traditionally, forms are documents with areas for a user to put information which is relevant to some purpose or another. Generally some sort of transaction is taking place, with the user providing data to accomplish a goal.

Forms are themselves a subtle form of communication and can reveal things about the person or institution asking the questions – nearly as much as they can about those who fill them in.

Forms in HTML are made up of fields for types of data. The best forms have labels to tell the user what the data should be, and some even have a placeholder which gives a further illustration of the structure of that data. Following is an example of an email **input**, and Figure 3.1 shows the output of the code.

```
<form>
  <label for="email">
    Email Address:
  </label>
<input
  type="email"
  name="email"
  placeholder="example@domain.com"/>
</form>
```

Figure 3.1 A simple email form

Email Address: example@domain.com

There are very many types of form input, and the number of types increased markedly after the introduction of HTML5. Not all types of input are supported by all browsers, though, and often their implementation can be markedly different across browsers and devices. Examples of the most common types of input are:

- **text:** for inputting a single line of text;
- **password:** for inputting a password – the entered text is often obfuscated or hidden in some way, usually by replacing the characters with asterisk or star characters;
- **submit:** for submitting form data to a form handler;
- **radio:** allows the user to select a single option from several available options;
- **checkbox:** defines a binary option – the value can either be true or false.

Alongside inputs, there are two other elements which can be placed within forms: **textarea** and **select**. A **textarea** is used for the collection of multi-line text and can be enhanced to provide WYSIWYG-type inputs (see Chapter 1 for more on WYSIWYG), whereas **select** allows for similar functionality to be applied to **radio** inputs except that multiple options can be allowed with the use of the **multiple** attribute.

Labels and placeholders in forms

Why, you might ask, is there an instance of **label** as well as **placeholder** in the code above? The subject of placeholders and labels is contentious, with some suggesting that using one or the other is fine and using both is overkill.

In the example above, the label and placeholder serve different purposes, with the label telling the user what is expected and the placeholder giving an example of the value required. There are many instances where you will see the placeholder used as a label, but this is questionable.

Labels are essential for many reasons. Clicking on a label places the focus on the input and, in the case of checkbox inputs, toggles the state of the input.

As a front-end developer, I often click on the text beside checkbox inputs (i.e. asking if I would like to opt out of marketing when creating an account on a website) rather than the input itself in the expectation that my choices will be respected, only to have to click the much smaller input, as what I was expecting to be the label was just text. This choice of replacing a semantic element with simple text makes no sense.

Assistive technologies, such as screen readers, use labels to understand the meaning of inputs. While most users are likely to be able to understand the context of the input from the other content within the page, many assistive technologies read out the text of the label related to the input. The label should describe in sufficient detail what input is required from the user. This is another reason why using labels is essential.

It once was fashionable to omit labels altogether in favour of placeholders but, as pointed out by the Nielsen Norman Group, this led to significant issues:

Placeholder text within a form field makes it difficult for people to remember what information belongs in a field, and to check for and fix errors. It also poses additional burdens for users with visual and cognitive impairments. (Sherwin, 2018)

Thankfully this was a short-lived fad. I can understand why using placeholders instead of labels is attractive, as it reduces the screen real-estate required for forms while assuming that a placeholder might fulfil the same purpose as a label. However, as we can see, this is not the case (W3C, 2011).

While placeholders can provide specific advice for users, labels should be your default option for inputs, though this conclusion also raises a further area of contention – that of the placement of the labels.

Traditionally, paper-based forms had the label placed on the top left above the field it was associated with, and users are used to this convention. There are, though, places where forms work differently, with the label being to the left, sometimes with further information beneath, and the input is on the right of the page. This type of form layout might seem to be a clear way to offer users full and proper prompting for the information required without having to have large amounts of horizontal space between inputs, but studies have shown that following the convention is easier for users (Wroblewski, 2005).

Fieldset and legend in forms
Along with the label–input pairing, there is another pairing of elements worth bearing in mind concerning forms, that of the `fieldset` and `legend`. The `fieldset` element is used to group related inputs, and the `legend` acts as a label for those fields so grouped. It is implemented mainly on long forms but seems to be less prevalent than it once was, mostly because forms are getting smaller and being split into multiple pages, so the need to separate distinct areas of a form has been replaced with the use of separate subforms.

Validation
Validation is essential for form fields. It is carried out before a form is submitted and ensures that the data requested for

a form is complete and that it has been entered in the correct format.

Browers are catching up with native implementations of most methods of validation using a Boolean attribute. A Boolean attribute indicates something when it exists on an element, even without a value. There are a few Boolean attributes, and adding them via JavaScript can sometimes be problematic because when adding attributes via JavaScript it is usual to give the attribute and then the new value.[7] These attributes include **required**,[8] **checked**[9] and **disabled**[10] (Schouten, 2015).

In the email input code example above, to make use of the browser's built-in validation, we would write the HTML like this:

```
<input type="email"
       name="email"
       placeholder="example@domain.com"
       required/>
```

The above code represents an input of the type **email**. It has a name – **email** – which will be sent to the form handler and gives a visual indication to the user of what type of information it will require in the form of an example email address. It is also a required input.

This browser-based validation can cope with many, but not all, use cases. For instance, if we need to check a telephone number, we can make an input of type **tel**, as in this example

---

7 There is a fascinating discussion of this issue on Stack Overflow (see Stack Overflow, 2019). The first answer is particularly enlightening.

8 **Required** indicates that the input must have a value. It works with the following input types: **text**, **search**, **url**, **tel**, **email**, **password**, **date pickers**, **number**, **checkbox**, **radio** and **file**.

9 **Checked** indicates whether the input is pre-selected. It works with the following input types: **checkbox** and **radio**.

10 **Disabled** indicates whether an input is disabled and will prevent its submission to the form handler. It can be useful to ensure that a previous condition has been met before allowing input.

from MDN Web Docs (formerly the Mozilla Developer Network) (Mozilla, 2019c):

```
<label for="phone">
  Enter your phone number:
</label>
<input
  type="tel"
  id="phone"
  name="phone"
  pattern="[0-9]{3}-[0-9]{3}-[0-9]{4}"
  required/>
<span class="note">
  Format: 123-456-7890
</span>
```

As you can see, the input has a **pattern** attribute which has a regular expression indicating a phone number from the USA. In this case, the accompanying **span** shows an example of valid input, but this is not a valid format for a UK phone number (Sandeepsure, 2012); validation becomes confusing for internationally formatted phone numbers.

There are pitfalls of validating a phone number, but addresses can be even more problematic. There is, however, an International Organization for Standardization (ISO) standard (ISO 19160 (International Cartographic Association, 2017)), which defines a conceptual model and associated terms and definitions, providing for the conversion of address information between specifications. Addresses within the UK are, compared to some jurisdictions, a breeze, with a house number and postal code often being enough to find an address – though those who live in less conventional accommodation, such as boats, can find this convention problematic.

Despite the perils of validation, keep in mind that we are here to help our users interact with our work. Often developers have invested significant time in becoming familiar with a JavaScript validation framework, such as the jQuery Validation Plugin (Arkni & Staab, 2018), and are reticent about using the native capabilities of the browser. Despite constraint validation being available, they can seem to prefer shoe-horning their own, preferred method rather than take advantage of the capabilities of the browser. Such non-standard validation can leave users confused, and the addition of further JavaScript can have an impact on page-load times.

Quite apart from validation in the browser, we should be conscious that the server should also validate all responses – if only to ensure that no malicious content is saved in the database. The W3C goes into far greater depth on this issue in its article on SQL injection (W3Schools, 2020c).

In his article 'HTML Forms' Time Has Come (Again)', George Mauer (2017) points to a lack of browser-side validation as being one of the primary reasons why forms became unpopular for a period.

Despite all this contention around forms, they will doubtless play a significant part in your career. Bear in mind the advice from the Web Accessibility Initiative (W3C, 2019) when thinking about forms: making forms accessible for users with disabilities only improves the experience for all your users and will improve the semantics[11] of your page, allowing it to be useful to software agents.[12]

Layouts

Once we know what we need to show our users, we need to decide how we should display it – how we should arrange the

---

[11] Semantics is all about the meaning of words. If a form is well structured semantically (e.g. with form inputs organised into groups which make sense), then it is far easier to understand what is required. This is best illustrated by thinking about forms that ask for an address. They usually have a structure which asks for First Line, Second Line, City/Town, State/Province/Region, Zip/Postal Code and finally Country. This semantic grouping is something you will doubtless see frequently, and placing a Phone Number input between any of the above inputs would be semantically jarring.

[12] A software agent is a program that acts on behalf of a user, such as Alexa (Amazon), Cortana (Microsoft), Siri (Apple) or Google's Assistant.

various elements on the page appropriately and pleasingly. This is the layout.

Table-based layouts

As I have mentioned, HTML was initially designed for the presentation of academic documents. Tables and tabular data played a significant part in these documents, and we can imagine a nascent designer seeing tables and thinking that they might offer a simple way of arranging content on a page.

Tables lent themselves to the archetypal two-column layout with header and footer so beloved of designers. Such a design is easy to create using a table-based layout, which explains why it was as popular as it was for many years.

The following is a simple example of a table-based layout:

```
<table>
    <tr>
        <td colspan="2" class="header"></td>
    </tr>
    <tr>
        <td class="sidebar"></td>
        <td class="content"></td>
    </tr>
    <tr>
        <td colspan="2" class="footer"></td>
    </tr>
</table>
```

It can be combined with this CSS:

```
table {
    width: 100%;
    border-collapse: collapse;
}
.header {
    background: #808080;
    height: 20px;
    width: 100%;
}
```

```
.sidebar {
    background: #DCDCDC;
    height: 50px;
    width: 25%;
}
.content {
    background: #000000;
    height: 20px;
    width: 75%;
}
.footer {
    background: #A9A9A9;
    height: 20px;
}
```

Together, they produce a layout with a grey header, 20px tall; a left-hand sidebar, which is the colour gainsboro,[13] 50px tall and 25% the width of the table; a content area which is black and takes up the remaining space (75%), also 50px tall; and a grey footer, 20px tall.

Figure 3.2 A simple table layout

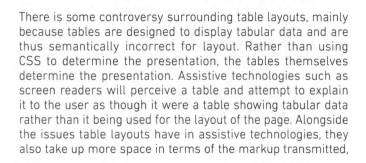

There is some controversy surrounding table layouts, mainly because tables are designed to display tabular data and are thus semantically incorrect for layout. Rather than using CSS to determine the presentation, the tables themselves determine the presentation. Assistive technologies such as screen readers will perceive a table and attempt to explain it to the user as though it were a table showing tabular data rather than it being used for the layout of the page. Alongside the issues table layouts have in assistive technologies, they also take up more space in terms of the markup transmitted,

---

13 A light grey colour.

and they prevent incremental rendering of the page, so the user has to wait longer to see anything on the page.

It is not only assistive technologies which have issues with tables, as search engines also use similar techniques to parse the page and extract relevant content. If a page is not parsed correctly by a search agent, then the indexing of the page will suffer. This is an issue with table-based layouts because a search agent is likely to try to read a table layout as though it were tabular data, in the order in which a table would be read – while the table layout might have the pertinent search data nested in a difficult-to-find place.

Making a page accessible has been described as the hallmark of a professional developer (Kyrnin, 2018). Eli Weinstock-Herman, in his article 'The History of HTML Table Layouts', uses this analogy to describe the issue:

> Building a house is hard. Can the house builder cut corners to get your house up faster? Sure. But at the end of the day, if the builder is professional they won't cut corners because those cut corners reduce the value of the house, reduce the satisfaction of the buyer, and increase the ongoing maintenance costs. (Weinstock-Herman, 2011)

Table-based layouts should also be avoided due to maintenance difficulties. Even though tables might seem like an easy win, they can quickly become a nightmare to maintain, and they perform worse than CSS-based layouts.

Quite apart from all these caveats of using table-based layouts, they are also prohibited, if not frowned upon, by the standards to which we should be working. For instance, the HTML 4.01 specification stated:

> Tables should not be used purely as a means to layout document content as this may present problems when rendering to non-visual media. Additionally, when used with graphics, these tables may force users to scroll horizontally to view a table designed on a system with a

larger display. To minimize these problems, authors should use style sheets to control layout rather than tables. (W3C, 1999)

HTML5 does not prohibit the use of table layout if the HTML is valid, but it does discourage it, saying that 'tables should not be used as layout aids' (W3C, 2017b). Now we know how not to lay out a page, what alternatives exist?

CSS-based layouts
As developers are strongly discouraged, if not actively prohibited, from using table layouts, they have instead moved to use CSS to produce the same results.

Replacing tables with CSS layouts   To start with, those wanting to replace tables with CSS layouts had recourse to the `float` and `display`[14] properties. These worked well but could be finicky and confusing initially. Using floats was the primary method of replacing table-based layouts for a long time, and it is worth understanding why and what pitfalls could trip up front-end developers while creating them.

The `float` attribute specifies how an element should float within its container. To understand them, it is worth thinking about how pages are structured with `div` HTML elements. The `div` element is used to signify a division of content so, for example, the two-column header and footer example provided earlier could be represented using four divisions within the `body` element of the HTML. Usually, these four `div` elements would have appropriately named `id` or `class` attributes such as `header`, `sidebar`, `content` and `footer`. These would then be targeted by the relevant CSS to prevent their default display one after the other. Note that the `div` element defaults to displaying as a block, which stretches the full width of the viewport and stretches vertically only as much as is required by the content of the `div`.

---

14 `Display` specifies the display behaviour of an element. Refer to W3Schools (2020a) for more information.

Using floats, we could pretty much ignore the **header**; give the **sidebar** a defined width and float it to the left; give the **content** a width, which when combined with the width of the **sidebar** would total less than the page width, and float it to the right; and direct the **footer** to **clear**[15] both.

This can be illustrated using this HTML:

```
<div class="header"></div>
<div class="sidebar"></div>
<div class="content"></div>
<div class="footer"></div>
```

And this CSS:

```
.header {
    background: #808080;
    height: 20px;
}
.sidebar {
    background: #DCDCDC;
    height: 50px;
    width: 25%;
    float: left;
}
.content {
    background: #000000;
    height: 50px;
    width: 75%;
    float: right;
}
.footer {
    background: #A9A9A9;
    height: 20px;
    clear: both;
}
```

---

15 In CSS settings, the **clear** property specifies on which side of an element floating elements can float.

From these, we get an identical layout to the table layout shown in Figure 3.2 with a significant saving of markup and reduced complexity. Rather than directing the `div` elements `sidebar` and `content` to float either left or right, it is possible to float both elements to the left and wrap them within a container `div` element with the `overflow` property set to `hidden` (this increases the amount of markup by adding an extra container; as you start to examine other developers' markup, you will gain an appreciation of simplicity and elegance – not least if you have to edit it later):

```css
.header {
    background: #808080;
    height: 20px;
}
.main {
    overflow: hidden;
}
.sidebar {
    background: #DCDCDC;
    height: 50px;
    width: 25%;
    float: left;
}
.content {
    background: #000000;
    height: 50px;
    width: 75%;
    float: left;
}
.footer {
    background: #A9A9A9;
    height: 20px;
    clear: both;
}
```

Using the `float` property is one way of replacing table-based layouts. Another is to use the `position` property, but it does require slightly more CSS:

```css
.header {
    background: #808080;
    height: 20px;
    position: absolute;
    top: 0;
    left: 0;
    width: 100%;
}
.sidebar {
    background: #DCDCDC;
    height: 50px;
    position: absolute;
    width: 25%;
    top: 20px;
    left: 0;
}
.content {
    background: #000000;
    height: 50px;
    position: absolute;
    width: 75%;
    top: 20px;
    right: 0;
}
.footer {
    background: #A9A9A9;
    height: 20px;
    position: absolute;
    width: 100%;
    top: 70px;
    right: 0;
}
```

This use of absolute positioning can be useful but it does not consider differing viewports, as it relies on the developer being specific. In the CSS above we see that the element with the **class** of **header** is precisely placed with its top-left corner on the top left of the viewport, with it being 20px high and 100% of the width of the page. The element with the **class** of **sidebar** has its top-left corner placed 20px down from the top left of the page, and is 50px tall and 25% the width of the page.

The element with the **class** of **content** is placed beside the element with the **class** of **sidebar**, with its top-left corner being 20px down and 25% of the page width from the left-hand side – it is 75% of the page width and 50px tall. The element with the **class** of **footer** has its top-left corner towards the left of the page and 70px down (20px for the element with the **class** of **header** and 50px for the element with the **class** of **sidebar**); like the element with the **class** of **header**, it is 100% of the page width.

There are likely more nuanced approaches to using absolute-relative positioning, and I encourage you to look at the useful resource developed by BarelyFitz Designs (2006). This tutorial provides an intuitive and informative way of learning CSS positioning in ten steps. When I first started, I spent a great deal of time reminding myself of the rules with this tutorial.

There is a way of getting back to the table effect with CSS should one desire; we can persuade HTML elements to display as though they were elements within a table using the **display** property:

```
<div class="table">
    <div class="header"> </div>
    <div class="row-with-content">
        <div class="sidebar"> </div>
        <div class="content"> </div>
    </div>
    <div class="footer"> </div>
</div>
```

The above HTML could use the following CSS to get our layout using the **display** property:

```
.table {
    display: table;
    width: 100%;
}
```

```
.row-with-content {
    display: table;
    width: 100%;
}
.header {
    background: #808080;
    height: 20px;
    display: table-row;
    width: 100%;
}
.sidebar {
    background: #DCDCDC;
    height: 50px;
    display: table-cell;
    width: 25%;
}
.content {
    background: #000000;
    height: 20px;
    display: table-cell;
    width: 75%;
}
.footer {
    background: #A9A9A9;
    height: 20px;
}
```

This sort of gets around the issue of having table layouts, by getting the browser to treat our elements as though they were table elements, but there are limitations regarding a lack of **colspan** and **rowspan** equivalents.

The **colspan** attribute defines the number of columns a cell should span, and a **rowspan** attribute specifies the number of rows a cell should span.

The **colspan** attribute is used twice in the example I gave at the beginning of this section on table-based layouts, once for the header and again for the footer. As such, the example in this box required extra markup to mimic the float and position layout equivalents – nearly as much markup as the table layout.

Using such a pseudo-table layout is not something I would recommend, but it is worth knowing as it might come in useful at some point if only to decipher CSS written by someone else. I would suggest it as an alternative to float- or position-based layouts only if you do not have access to more modern techniques and need your solution to work in non-evergreen browsers.

Modern layouts The layout methods detailed above illustrate something of the history of CSS layout techniques. We will now examine the two more modern approaches to layout, which will be the ones you will likely be tasked with implementing: flexbox and grid.

Flexbox layouts CSS-based layouts were a huge improvement over table layouts but are still limited in terms of their use in mobile devices, such as phones or tablets; using percentages and fixed widths in the way that they do means that information can become illegible. A more modern layout approach requires a little more markup but will likely prove to be much more flexible.

Consider the following HTML:

```
<div class="header"></div>
<div class="main">
    <div class="sidebar"></div>
    <div class="content"></div>
</div>
<div class="footer"></div>
```

with the following CSS:

```
.header {
    background: #808080;
    height: 20px;
}
.main {
    display: flex;
}
.sidebar {
    background: #DCDCDC;
    height: 50px;
    flex: 1;
}
.content {
    background: #000000;
    height: 50px;
    flex: 3;
}
.footer {
    background: #A9A9A9;
    height: 20px;
}
```

This code uses the flexbox-layout module, which provides an efficient way to lay out, align and distribute space among items in a container, without being overly concerned about their content. This allows for responsive layouts.

The flexbox-layout module has several features and allows the developer to control several aspects of the initial layout as well as providing rules which enable better placement of content within different devices, such as mobile phones or tablets. The developer can control the direction of the flow of elements within a container such that any cardinal direction is possible (left to right, right to left, top to bottom or bottom to top). The ordering of the elements can also be controlled, as can their wrapping behaviour in smaller containers – with that wrapping being either horizontal or vertical. Further elements can grow or shrink depending on the available space, and their alignment can be controlled within their container.

Flexbox layouts are concerned with one dimension, either horizontal or vertical. Flexbox rules are made up of two main components:

- **The flexbox container:** setting the `display` property of an element to *flex* is enough to invoke the flexbox rules, and the element will align to fit the available space and place child elements in the associated `flex-direction` (*row*, *row-reverse*, *column* or *column-reverse*). Although flexbox is associated with one dimension, elements can wrap should children take up more than the available space, and we have some control over this wrapping with the `flex-wrap` rule.

- **The flex items:** while the flexbox container is in charge of the general layout of the elements it contains, the elements themselves are in charge of their display and can have an initial size and an ability to grow and shrink by making use of the space within the flex-container using `flex-basis`, `flex-grow` and `flex-shrink`.

Flexbox is fast becoming the standard layout system, but it can be daunting for those who are used to older layout systems. There are many resources available to help the developer to learn it, such as Flexbox Froggy (http://flexboxfroggy.com).

Grid layouts   Closely aligned to flexbox layouts are grid layouts. According to the web developer and blogger Chris Coyier:

> Flexbox layout is most appropriate to the components of an application, and small-scale layouts, while the Grid layout is intended for larger scale layouts. (Coyier, 2018)

The two have very similar syntax, and, in the case of grid layouts, they can be massaged into playing nicely with earlier browsers, such as Internet Explorer 11 (probably the earliest browser you will be asked to support). Following is the equivalent CSS to the flexbox example above using a grid layout:

```
.header {
    background: #808080;
    height: 20px;
}
.main {
    display: grid;
    grid-template-columns: repeat(4, 1fr);
    height: 50px;
}
.sidebar {
    background: #DCDCDC;
    grid-column: 1;
}
.content {
    background: #000000;
    grid-column: 2 / 5;
}
.footer {
    background: #A9A9A9;
    height: 20px;
}
```

One thing to take note of above is the use of the **fr** unit. It represents a fraction of the leftover space in a grid container (W3C, 2017a), so the above code splits the area of the container into four equally spaced segments. The **fr** unit can also be used to measure the vertical space within a container, and this ability, along with the fact that developers can mix and match units, means that the grid-layout method is infinitely flexible.

Grid is the fifth technique I have had to learn to produce the same result. It is the one that seems to me to be the most exciting and, after struggling to get it working with Internet Explorer 11 (Myers, 2018b), it is the one I feel most comfortable using and supporting going forward.

It must be noted that Internet Explorer 11 has a non-standard approach to CSS grid layouts, and so investigating a polyfill[16] or learning its peculiarities is worthwhile.

In much the same way as flexbox layouts have two main elements, so too do grid layouts:

- **The grid container:** again, setting the `display` property of an element to *grid* generates a block-level grid (setting it to *inline-grid* generates an inline-level grid for use in flow-based layouts). Setting the `display` to grid is only useful when we define the columns and rows using `grid-template-columns` and `grid-template-rows` rules or even the `grid-template` rule. We can also specify a gap between child elements using the `grid-gap` rule[17] as well as align items along both directions and align the grid within its parent container. As you can probably imagine, with their ability to control a two-dimensional grid, the rules associated with grid containers are extensive. CSS-Tricks has produced an excellent resource on this (CSS-Tricks, 2020).

- **The grid items:** the primary rules associated with grid elements deal with how they are placed within their parent's grid container and are associated with which grid and column they should start in and which grid or column cell they should stretch to. These rules allow for fine control over their placement, but note that the numbering system starts from 1 rather than from 0, which is what you will become used to once you are proficient with JavaScript. Again, I refer you to the resource from CSS-Tricks (2020) for more information.

---

16 A polyfill is a plugin or piece of code that provides the technology that a browser should provide.

17 Though not in Internet Explorer 11.

The grid rows and columns can be named within any template rules you create on the grid container. This will help your understanding of the placement of elements within the grid.

Discussion of flexbox and grid   Throughout this section, we have looked at how layouts can be accomplished using several CSS techniques and finished off by looking at both the flexbox and grid layouts. These are becoming by far the most popular methods of laying out pages, so we spent a little time introducing both. It should be noted, though, that there is a fundamental difference between them. Flexbox is made for one-dimensional layouts, whereas grid is made for two-dimensional layouts. To put this another way, a flexbox can be either a row or a column, whereas a grid layout can be both rows and columns. We do have the ability to wrap elements within flexbox containers to ensure that those elements which do not fit within the single dimension wrap into another *row* or *column*, but we do not have the fine-grained control offered by grid layouts.

When it comes to deciding whether you should use one or the other, I would instead suggest using both, as they complement each other. Grid can be used predominantly to build the scaffolding of websites and flexbox can be used to structure the elements contained within the scaffold. To summarise: learn both and use them together.

Final thoughts on layouts

We have seen several ways of generating the same design using different techniques, but by far the most useful are the more modern flexbox and grid layouts. I encourage you to familiarise yourself with the others as well, as there might be a place for them in your practice. However, despite Internet Explorer 11's non-standard implementation of grid, flexbox and grid should be your primary tools going forward as they will help you to create responsive layouts.

Tables

The previous section mentioned something of the chequered past of tables on the internet. Using tables for layout was a necessary part of the evolution of the internet. However, now that CSS techniques have removed the need to use them for layout, we can reuse them for their proper – if not traditional – purpose: displaying tabular data.

Like the `html` element, the `table` element should have at least a head and a body, but these can be supplemented with a foot, so a table element can have a `thead` (a table header) and a `tfoot` (a table footer), and should have a `tbody` (a table body). While a proper table should have at least a `thead` and a `tbody`, tables which omit both will still render correctly, due to browser manufacturers appreciating the abuse tables were subjected to in the past.

Tables are used to represent two-dimensional, tabular data – that is, data which is suited to display within rows and columns because it shares some common characteristics. For example, we could show the people with perfect Pac-Man scores on a particular day, as each person who has managed this shares some attributes, namely that they scored 3,333,360 in Pac-Man, they have a name, they scored on a specific date and they took a specified period to achieve their score. This data lends itself to display in a tabular format because we have our headings in place already. We can use 'Name', 'Date' and 'Time' as the text for our table header (`th`) elements in the `thead`, and we can duplicate the same arrangements of cells within the `tfoot` as well. Thus, each person would be represented within the table as a row and each attribute as a column.

The following is a minimal table of two records:

```
<table>
  <thead>
    <tr>
      <th>Name</th>
      <th>Year</th>
      <th>Hours</th>
    </tr>
  </thead>
  <tbody>
    <tr>
      <td>Billy Mitchell</td>
      <td>1983</td>
      <td>6</td>
    </tr>
    <tr>
      <td>Dave Race</td>
      <td>2013</td>
      <td>3</td>
    </tr>
  </tbody>
</table>
```

This produces the table shown in Figure 3.3.

_____

Figure 3.3 A simple table

Name	Year		Hours
Billy Mitchell	1983	6	
Dave Race	2013	3	

For completeness sake, we should add a **tfoot** to the table just beneath the **thead** and above the **tbody** (to allow rendering of the **tfoot** while the browser is still processing the table data (Network Working Group, 1996)). However, let's first look at the other elements used in the table.

Rows are signified using the **tr** (table-row) element, but within the **tr** we have either **th** (table-header) or **td** (table-data) elements.

th elements are not limited to use within the **thead**. A row can also have a **th** element, usually to denote some column of the row being of importance. So, in our example, the name of the person scoring could be a **th** instead of a **td**. It is also worth noting that the **thead** element can hold multiple rows, which can ease the layout – for instance, denoting a grouping of **th** elements under a shared category can be accomplished in this way.

Both the **td** and **th** elements can span multiple rows and columns, something which we looked at earlier when examining table layouts. For instance, if we had a table of orders with one column for unit price, another for units ordered and the last for a total (unit price multiplied by the number of units ordered), the last row might contain totalled numbers. We might not be interested in the total number of items ordered and we certainly gain nothing from a total of the individual prices of single units; however, if we were to total the total row values, then we could have the total of the whole order. We could have empty cells under the unit price and the units ordered, or we could remove those three cells and replace them with one cell with a **colspan** of 3, perhaps right-aligning the contents of the cell, as shown in Figure 3.4.

Figure 3.4 A simple table with a total of the row totals

Item	Cost	Amount		Total
Widget	£12.99	2		£25.98
Gadget	£9.99	3		£29.97
			Total:	£55.95

We should perhaps employ the same convention used within spreadsheets and make sure that all cells with numbers are right aligned. This helps our users to parse the numbers and aids them in totalling the numbers in their head (Brocka, 2012).

Tables can also contain other optional elements aside from those listed above. These include:

- **caption:** this, if present, should be the first element within the table and is the title of the table.

- **colgroup**: this should appear, if present, after the caption and before the main content of the table (i.e. the **thead**, **tbody** and **tfoot**). As you might be able to imagine from the name, it describes a group of one or more columns and should contain one or more **span** or **col** elements. These are primarily associated with the visual formatting of the data and are useful because they can be used to apply such formatting to multiple columns of data at once.

Probably due to the previous misuse of tables, they can have multiple attributes which have now almost totally been replaced by CSS directives. Most of these attributes are unsupported in HTML5, but you will see them used. Perhaps the most common ones are **cellpadding**, **cellspacing** and **border**. CSS can be used to replace these attributes, leaving much cleaner markup. A **padding** CSS directive can replace the **cellpadding** attribute, and **border-spacing** can be used instead of **cellspacing**.

One of the best ways of enhancing tables is DataTables (Jardine, 2018), but there are many others. DataTables can sort tables on one or more arbitrary columns, and provide sensible ordering on the type of data, such as ordering dates sequentially.

This ability of DataTables to cope with dates is by no means as simple as you might think, as dates are presented in all sorts of odd ways. As a front-end developer, you will likely become, if you are not already, adept at being able to parse dates entered by users from other regions of the world from your own.

For me at least, understanding US-formatted dates was a huge pain, but I can cope as I see them so frequently. DataTables also allows for the filtering of rows using either a regular expression or simple text. Additionally, being able to use pagination so that users are not presented with long tables is brilliant, as is being able to offload the heavy lifting to the server when using pagination so that only the visible data is within the structure of the page.

Whichever table enhancement you choose to adopt, if any, be aware that you might have to cope with making sure it will work with whatever framework you are using at the time (Angular, React, Vue or whatever else arises). This flexibility is by no means always clear cut, as I personally still include jQuery despite it being less and less necessary, just so that I can continue to use DataTables.

I imagine that these enhancements to the HTML table element may well be addressed natively in the future. The standard certainly seems to be suggesting that, as it was only in 2016 that the sortable and sorted attributes were removed from the draft specification for HTML5.1 (Faulkner, 2016). However, until browsers support such abilities natively, we will have to use JavaScript.

Images

Front-end developers are rarely tasked with creating images, but it is worth understanding them because they will make up much of your working life. Front-end developers are often asked to use images within the application either as decoration or for illustrative purposes. Being a front-end developer means being engaged in a creative process, whether you appreciate your inner artist or not. Who knows, if you do not already dabble in the creation of art, you may well find yourself drawn to it in the future – if only to supplement any designs a designer or client might provide you with.

Images are used for many purposes within HTML: to create an atmosphere or feeling, to help explain a concept, to identify people, places or objects, and even to reinforce the message contained within the text or build brand loyalty.

Raster images

Raster images are composed of pixels, quite often lots and lots of pixels. Each can be a different colour from its neighbouring pixel. Raster images can also be called bitmaps.

When it comes to digital images, the artist starts with a blank canvas. However, in the context of raster images, there is a multitude of choices about the canvas itself. A conventional artist has some questions they must answer before ever putting an image on a canvas. Do they have a defined palette of colours with which to work? What are the dimensions of the canvas? What media (such as paintbrushes, airbrushes, pen, pencil or a combination of any of them) will be used?

In the realm of the front-end, these choices are duplicated except for the choice of media. In our purview, media might best be equated with software, as different programs are suited to the production of different types of image.

It might be that you have an image for inclusion in the project you are developing but it requires some tweaking. These tweaks can take myriad different forms: the image might be the wrong size for the container it needs to fill, it might be the wrong aspect ratio[18] or (and this is my all-time least favourite

---

18 The ratio of the width to the height of an image. It is expressed as two numbers separated by a colon such that an image with an aspect ratio of 16:9 describes proportions which are 16 units wide and 9 units tall (the actual units do not matter in a ratio).

issue) it might have a background colour which needs to be changed. Let's look at how we can address these issues.

Image size and aspect ratio issues   If an image is the wrong aspect ratio, we can address this problem in two ways. We might edit the image in an external editor to ensure it is correct or we might employ CSS. Using CSS has the advantage of ensuring the image remains unsullied, but we might lose detail which the designer is hoping to convey, by accidentally trimming off the relevant detail. Editing the image is likely to be more precise and will allow you to ensure that it has been made suitable for inclusion by shrinking the resolution to that of its container. For instance, we might have a container which is 200px wide and 100px tall but be supplied with an image that is 2,000px wide and 1,000px tall. While the browser is capable of shrinking the image, we have transferred a significantly larger image than that which is required over the network; it would be far better to supply the image in the desired dimensions initially.

Background colour   Very rarely do images fit a square or rectangular shape (there are of course exceptions), and filling the whole four-sided canvas is quite rare. That means that the person creating the image is left with a problem, and that problem is what colour to put behind the thing which is depicted. Artists using traditional media do not always have quite the same problem because the media itself often has a colour, but digital artists can have a background or not – a little like a traditional artist painting on either an opaque or a transparent surface.

Imagine a logo for a company. How does one display that within an HTML document? We looked at the `img` element when we looked at HTML in Chapter 2, but what about the actual image itself? We know that, if it is a raster image, it will be a quadrilateral made up of some individual pixels of different colours. The colour of the underlying container is a given and will, generally, be associated with the overall theme of the site, so the designer may well opt to use the same colour as the background for the logo.

However, what if, for example, next year the designer goes on maternity leave and another designer is brought in. They may choose to put their stamp on the company design and change the hue of the theme. As a consequence you, as a front-end developer, may be tasked with updating the theme across the whole web estate of the company. You tweak the CSS and dig down into the minutiae of the JavaScript to change any variables there to reflect the new coloration. It takes a significant amount of time to ensure you have caught all references to the old colour and replaced them with the new hex value (more of which later), but you finally think you are ready to test your changes in the browser. Everything looks good, except for one glaring instance which is visible on every page: the logo. All your hard work is for nought as there is a discordant image on each page; the original designer did not envisage the theme colour changing and so used it as the background to the logo. She is not available, nor are the assets she used in the creation of the logo, and, besides, the source for the image is a Photoshop file, and you do not have a licence for it.

In a situation like this, you can fire up Gimp[19] (GIMP, 2018) and, if you need to, frantically search for tutorials on how to remove a background from an image (Viola, 2012). Once the original background has been removed, you are left in something of a quandary: whether to leave the background transparent or add the new background colour. You assume that the original designer will not be away from work forever and that the current designer might not be in place when she returns, so it might be best to back up the original and replace it with a new image with the new colour. You could also remove the background colour and allow the underlying colour to show through the transparent areas of the image. What you decide to do will depend upon the format of the image. Some image formats support transparency, and some support multiple types of transparency.

---

19 Gimp is an open-source image editor and alternative to Photoshop.

Some image formats do not support transparency at all, and these are generally the formats used to display photographs. Photographs are pictures of real, concrete things such as products, people or locations. As such, there is no need for transparency, as the image is flat. When we are not displaying photographs, though, we can make use of transparency.

In the old days, there was a single format which supported transparency, and that was the Graphics Interchange Format (GIF), developed in 1987. Nowadays we have a much more nuanced approach to transparency with other formats.

GIF images are brilliant, though. They are primarily dominant because of the compression they use to generate quite small files, and this means that each pixel has a colour, one of which can be transparent.

A powerful aspect of GIF is its ability to be used for animation. This ability to contain numerous frames and data on display is perhaps the primary reason for GIFs' continued popularity, with sites such as Giphy.com allowing users to embed pertinent animations in a multitude of places.

That means that in our example scenario, we could convert the original logo to a GIF with transparency, and we should be fine. We should be aware, though, that our logo once had a background, and on the edges of the logo there will be artefacts of that background colour left behind because of the nature of raster images. In raster images, lines are not lines at all; instead, they are a collection of many squares which, at a distance, appear as though they are lines.

We are now nearly there. Nearly everything looks correct, and the old colour has been replaced throughout, except for the weird jagging around the logo, so what to do? First we need to understand how colours are represented digitally and why another image format – Portable Network Graphics (PNG) – might be preferable to GIF.

Vector images

We have looked at the issues associated with using raster images and how these issues lead to interesting solutions such as using alternative colour models (more of which later). This is primarily down to the fact that raster images are mainly designed to display pictures such as photographs. Photographs record light falling upon a surface and, in this aspect at least, they mimic the human eye. However, they are not appropriate for all images. In the case of the logo problem discussed earlier, the issue was the bounding line and the jagging surrounding it.

Vector graphics are made up of lines.

> I use the term 'graphics' in this context to distinguish images which are generated by a computer from visual representations of things. There is something of a blurring of this distinction, though, with many photographic images now having significant input from software.

Vector graphics are made up of two-dimensional points connected by lines or curves to form shapes. Whereas we can use Photoshop for raster images, we can use Adobe Illustrator for vector graphics. Those who are looking for alternatives can use Gimp and Inkscape for similar purposes. Inkscape uses the Scalable Vector Graphic (SVG) format natively.

SVG Initially, it was only possible to view SVG images using a browser plugin created by Adobe but in 2009 Internet Explorer 9 gained native support for the format. However, even the last iteration of Internet Explorer had issues with the scaling of SVG images (Deveria, n.d.-a) so supporting the format across all the major browsers requires some extra work, but the effort is well worth it to have vector graphics.

Working with SVG is very similar to working with HTML as the format makes use of angle brackets and elements in a similar way, which makes sense, as it is also XML-based. Where things get interesting, though, is that there are many different elements with many attributes which may well seem unfamiliar. It is outside the remit of this book to go into much detail on the minutiae of the format; however, there is a wealth of resources available. For advice on using SVG in your practice, I recommend you read Chris Coyier's *Practical SVG* (Coyier, 2016).

Including SVG within HTML can be problematic, though this situation was significantly eased by HTML5, which incorporates the ability to embed SVG directly in the HTML markup of a document (W3Schools, 2020d). Before HTML5, a SVG file could be referenced in the `src` attribute of an `img` element; it could also be referenced in the `data` attribute of an `object` element with a `type` attribute of `image/svg+xml`. One other alternative existed, and this was the `embed` element, with the SVG being referenced again within the `src` attribute. The `embed` element method is unusual as it is an element that was only added to the HTML standard with HTML5 but was used widely beforehand, as a *de facto* part of the standard for the inclusion of non-HTML content, such as audio. HTML5 also added `audio` and `video` elements, making their inclusion within HTML significantly less fraught unless the developer is working with older browsers unable to support HTML5.

In much the same way as raster images sometimes require some form of compression to not delay the user in their journey through an interaction with the product you are helping to develop, SVGs can become bloated. They are therefore compressed using GNU zip (GZIP) compression to produce SVGZ files, which are typically 50% to 80% smaller.

Scripting images   Where SVGs hold the crown, though, is that they can be scripted with JavaScript. Scripting means that not only can you use your text editor to create them (though internally visualising the final output can be tricky) but you can also use JavaScript to interact with the SVG document, allowing some quite complex and engaging visualisations to be produced. That is by no means the only option available when it comes to simple animation or styling of SVGs, though. As well as JavaScript, CSS and SMIL[20] can be used to animate SVGs, and Chris Coyier's *Practical SVG* (mentioned above) has a whole section comparing the methods.

That is not to say that the same cannot be done with raster graphics. With the introduction and widespread adoption of the `canvas` element, JavaScript gained the ability to interact with raster images. There are significant differences between the two technologies, but the front-end developer does have ways of generating dynamic illustrations using each.

We should investigate this a little more, though, as the philosophies of interacting with SVG images and `canvas` elements are profoundly different. Whereas we use JavaScript to interact with the document object model (DOM) of an SVG image by creating, editing or deleting objects within the DOM, canvas objects are drawn in an immediate mode, meaning that there is no opportunity to interrogate the canvas to see what is already there, so no editing is possible, excepting redrawing of the entire `canvas` element. We need to record the placement of elements within the JavaScript and, if a part of the image requires creation, editing or deletion, then the whole canvas has to be drawn. When I imagine this process, I think of stop-motion animation, but instead of using acetate sheets for the backgrounds, they would be stored within a JavaScript variable or function.

Embedding SVG images with HTML used to be a very complicated process but has been made very much easier as the standard has gained support. SVG markup can be placed directly inline in HTML5 documents but is perhaps best used with the `img` element, with the SVG file being the target of the

---

20 SMIL (pronounced 'smile') stands for Synchronized Multimedia Integration Language.

`src` attribute. You can also use the `object` or `embed` elements or reference the `img` within the HTML. The best way will depend on your use case and whether the SVG is interactive in some way. If it is, then using the `object` element or inline SVG would be the most suitable ways of including the SVG.

Just as we can use the `img` element to embed SVG files within HTML, we can also take advantage of the `picture` element. This element can contain multiple `source` elements and one `img` element to serve as a fallback should any of the offered `source` elements not be suitable. What I mean by this is that each `source` element can have a `media` attribute which will be evaluated – these are like CSS media queries (discussed in the previous chapter) – such that we can define a `min-width` (for instance). Then, if the `media` attribute evaluates to false, then the next `source` will be evaluated. As well as having an optional `media` attribute, the `source` can have a `type` attribute, and the two work together if the browser supports the MIME type[21] for images. If the `media` and optional `type` attributes evaluate to true, then the image within the `srcset` is used. The `srcset` attribute is a comma-separated list of image descriptors with each descriptor being made up of a URL to the image and either a width descriptor or a pixel density descriptor. The `picture` element is relatively new but very powerful, and allows you to have dedicated images for different browsers and devices.

In the same way that CSS has different measurement units suited to different purposes, there is no best image format. Both raster and vector have their uses in different contexts, and they are, if anything, complementary rather than incompatible.

Ways of representing colour
Hex values   Hex values are one of many ways of describing colours. They are formed of either three or six numbers, preceded by the hash symbol, and they represent colours using

---

21 Multipurpose Internet Mail Extension (MIME) is a standardised way of classifying file types on the internet. It is made up of two parts: a type and a subtype separated by a slash.

red, green and blue. In the case of three-digit hex values, each digit represents a single value; in the case of six-digit values, each grouping of two digits represents a value for red, green and blue with red being the first two digits after the hash symbol, green the second set of two and blue the final set of two digits.

Each set of one or two digits represents a number between 0 and 255, with single digits jumping every 16 numbers. This conversion between three-digit numbers (such as 255) and two-digit numbers (such as FF) is necessary because hex numbers, as you might be able to guess from the name, use the hexadecimal number base. This means that once we have run out of regular decimal numbers, we move on to letters. This progression goes 0, 1, 2, 3, 4, 5, 6, 7, 8, 9, A, B, C, D, E and F. In hex numbers that are three digits long, 0 means 0, 10 means 16 (11 hexadecimal means one 16 and one 1), 20 means 32 (22 hexadecimal means two 16s and two 1s, giving us 34), all the way up to FF, meaning 255[22] (FF hexadecimal means that we have access to 256 possible values as 0 is a valid value, so 0 through to 255 represents 256 possible integer – or whole number – values). It is important to note that using the three-digit shorthand reduces the number of possible colours to 4,096, whereas the six-digit notation allows for a palette of 16,777,216.

Hex is the primary method of representing colours that you will see during your professional life, but it is by no means the only method available to you. It is worth looking at the others available in CSS, such as the Hue, Saturation, Lightness (HSL) representation.

If you have a licence for Photoshop, it is worth investigating the colour models available in that program as some are fascinating – I especially like Cyan, Magenta, Yellow and Key (CMYK), but it is primarily used in print media.

---

22 This can be confusing, but we count digits including 0.

RGB and RGBA   Hex colours are part of the Red, Green, Blue (RGB) colour model, in which hexadecimal numbers represent the values for each colour. However, there are other ways of representing RGB colours. For instance, if you are uncomfortable using hexadecimal, it is also possible to use decimal integers (for example, `rgb(255, 0, 0)` is equivalent to `#FF0000`) or even percentages (`rgb(100%, 0%, 0%)`).

The RGB model did not, until the introduction of CSS3, support transparency. It does now, using the Red, Green, Blue and Alpha (RGBA) model, which introduced an extra, fourth, channel which indicates the degree of opacity of each pixel. Within CSS this fourth channel has a value between 0 and 1, with 0 being transparent and 1 being opaque so that a semi-transparent red would be described like this: `rgba(255, 0, 0, 0.5)`. More recent browsers can even use four- or eight-digit hex numbers to represent RGBA values; in this case, the same semi-transparent red would appear like this: `#FF000080`.

The RGBA model is the colour model used in the Portable Network Graphics (PNG) format (mentioned earlier) and will allow us to remove the background from the logo in our earlier example, without fear of artefacts showing from the previous background colour. Using the PNG format means that the lines which bound our logo can gradually taper off to transparency towards the edge rather than being blocks of solid colour, thus allowing any new background colour to seep through and removing the slight jagging we noted using the GIF format. Most raster editors are able to export images as PNGs.

JPEG and WebP   There are now more options available to us in terms of graphics formats, and even the trusty JPEG has seen some evolution with the introduction of Progressive JPEG, which alters the way JPEG images are displayed. Rather than rendering each pixel from the top of the image downwards, they instead initially render a lower-quality image which becomes more lavish in detail as the browser loads more of the picture.

A newer format is Google's WebP, which is smaller than equivalent PNG and JPEG images thanks to its use of a different encoding mechanism. Internet Explorer 11 is unable to support WebP, but polyfills provide older browser support. If you do not need to support anything other than evergreen browsers, WebP is a good choice as it also supports alpha transparency and is about 26% smaller in terms of file size, meaning that images load much faster.

Data visualisation

As a front-end developer, anything that helps your user to understand a process is an excellent idea, and visualisations can be a big part of that. Visualisations seek to distil pertinent information into a format that can be easily understood. It is essential to use words as well, though, especially for users with limited visual acuity.

You will doubtless see data visualisations every day yourself, even if only in mainstream media such as newspapers and TV news programmes. Indeed, many innovative methods of visualising data have come from such media – sometimes from their concrete manifestations, sometimes from their online portals.

Tables
We have looked at tables before and the place they have within the context of front-end development. Tables are one of the most elegant forms of visualisation, despite often not being recognised as such. Indeed, Kevin Dunn (2018) notes that the human eye cannot adequately decode angles (for instance, in pie charts), whereas we have minimal difficulty with linear data, such as that displayed within a table.

However, Mitch Daniels of Viget Labs notes that 'while our team loves the smell of a cleanly-formatted CSV [comma-separated values file], our clients are often... less enthused with that raw data. They recognise its value but staring at tables can make their eyes glaze over' (Daniels, 2016). He has a point, and this is a situation where it is worth bearing in mind our own biases and prior experiences.

I am not a spreadsheet guru, but the work I have done with DataTables means that I am more than happy with tabular data, no matter the delivery format. I delight in writing tools to gain further insights into this data using JavaScript, even going so far as to write methods through which arbitrary CSV (comma-separated values) files can be imported and displayed. Our users are probably not so experienced, though, or might be limited concerning the time they can invest scrolling through long data sets.

I caution against using other forms of data visualisation where a table would suffice. For instance, if you need to compare exact figures within a range for a specific row, a table is of far more use than a chart as there is no requirement to check the legend or the key – instead, the user can find the intersection of a column and row to see the value. Tables are also particularly helpful when it comes to comparing individual values and even different units of measurement. Their ultimate use, though, is in providing totals.

Charts
Despite my appreciation of tables, there are times when a relationship is only apparent when data is displayed in a chart. This is particularly the case when it comes to imagining the shape of the values within a data set, such as patterns, trends and exceptions. Charts are also invaluable when it comes to revealing relationships between whole sets of values – for example, to compare sales figures among teams.

I was once tasked with mapping the management structure of an NHS Trust and found a very complicated management structure, with people managed by multiple direct supervisors and sometimes-circular chains of responsibility. Exploring such a data set using a table would have been confusing but displaying it in a chart made the relationships obvious.

There are many charting libraries to choose from: D3 and Chart.js are just two examples. Your employer might have their preference and may well have opted to use a commercial library.

Doughnut charts and pie charts can be brilliant for displaying the relative proportions of multiple classes of data and for displaying a data set in a visual form. They also have the added benefit of being widely understood and requiring minimum additional explanation except for labels for the different wedges.

Stephen Few notes in his article 'Save the Pies for Dessert' (Few, 2007) that doughnut and pie charts can be confusing, as readers are often unable to distinguish similarly sized slices of the pie from each other. Sven Hamberg (2018) expands on this, showing that being able to differentiate between 29% and 33% (for example) in a pie chart can be difficult, with this difficulty exacerbated by the surrounding data within the set.

Where data sets are large or have similar values, it might be better to employ something like a bar chart to avoid any issues with distinguishing similar values, as can be the case with pie charts. Bar charts allow users to compare the length of the bars representing the data – or indeed height, should the chart be oriented vertically rather than horizontally. This enables users to ascertain the proportional values represented.

With advances in CSS, it might be possible to get away without using a library or your custom solution to make simple bar charts. Also, many online and offline productivity suites provide the facility to generate and export charts, so it may well be that the visualisation you choose to show will be in the form of an image produced in another program.

129

Bar charts can suffer from similar issues to pie charts, though. For example, in stacked bar charts,[23] it can be problematic to distinguish similarly sized bars. Robert Kosara, a research scientist at Tableau Software (2018), has written about the issues with stacked bar charts (Kosara, 2016) and compared stacked bar charts to pie charts. When a data set is employed to display a total value, it is easy to judge which bar is highest (or longest); where confusion can set in, though, is when a comparison is made of the constituents of those bars. Because they have different starting points, there can be visual confusion when the difference in values is slight, and when comparing segments of data across categories.

There are many other types of chart, including bullet charts, histograms, line charts, scatter plots and funnel charts, to name just a few. Each is suited to a different type of data. It might be that using multiple visualisations for the same data set is appropriate in that the user is then presented with the same data but can choose to view the chart which best suits them.

Server-side languages (such as PHP with the GD Graphics Library[24]) can be used to generate visualisations from the data stored on the server, and these can be cached to save making repeated requests for the same image. There are many visualisations which make use of concrete things you might see every day, such as traffic lights and gauges, and these can be fun to make yourself (Myers, 2010).

---

23 Like normal bar charts, stacked bar charts use bars to show differences within categories of data but are further made up of segments which represent different parts of the whole bar. For a more detailed explanation, see the article 'Understanding Stacked Bar Charts: The Worst or the Best?' by Vitaly Radionov (2017) who suggests that they can be concise and easy to read in comparison with some other ways of displaying similar data.

24 The GD Graphics Library can be used to dynamically create and manipulate images on the server.

I would suggest perusing blogs such as FlowingData (Yau, 2018) to see how statisticians, designers, data scientists and others are using visualisation to represent data in innovative ways.

Web analytics

As a front-end developer, you may not have to deal with web analytics, though more enlightened employers might ask you to tweak any code sent off to an analytics service on a specific page when a particular action is initiated by your users.

Web analytics might mean that you discover that a particular part of your application attracts many more visitors than another but that it is not easily accessible via the navigation of your application. This might enable you to make the area readily available and ease your users' journey.

The Web Analytics Association's Standards Committee defines web analytics as 'the measurement, collection, analysis and reporting of web data for purposes of understanding and optimizing web usage' (WAA Standards Committee, 2008).

Web analytics requires data, collected either via server logs[25] or from JavaScript tagging.[26] By far the most popular is the latter approach, but the server logs approach can also offer insights. Google has made significant inroads into making the use of JavaScript tagging the default choice, as it is highly customisable and accurate (Gawron, 2016). However, server logs can be useful in situations where a site handles

---

[25] A server log records all activities that have an impact on the back-end of the application. It can be conceived as being like sonar: echoes of what the user does are reflected within the server log. JavaScript tagging, however, offers a more accurate picture of what the user is doing, almost as if you can peer over their shoulder as they interact with the application.

[26] Snippets of JavaScript that collect data and send it to an analytics service from the website in which it is embedded.

sensitive information which should not be exposed to external services. Server logs can also be useful on older or more content-heavy websites, where it can be impractical to insert JavaScript tagging into each page. Such sites may benefit from implementing a web template engine[27] (Wikipedia, 2020a), as integrating JavaScript tagging into a template is trivial.

Once the data has been collected, it needs to be processed into usable information, such as by placing it within a table or some other visualisation. Though humans are usually excellent at noticing patterns, those patterns can sometimes get lost in the noise.

However the data is translated into information, it is used to develop key performance indicators (KPIs), which are in turn used to measure the performance of the application or website being analysed. To a greater or lesser extent, these KPIs are generally associated with conversion of user visits into actions, such as visitors making their way through an e-commerce site to finally make a purchase. However, they can also be associated with statistics such as the average order value of a transaction.

Once the KPIs have been developed, an online strategy is formulated which aims to make changes to improve the business' scores against the KPIs. You will see that each step in this four-step process (collection of data, processing of data into information, development of KPIs and formulation of an online strategy) is informed by the preceding and following steps. As a front-end developer, you will likely play a part in each stage of this process, perhaps being asked to implement code that records a user's journey through some or all of the application. You might then be asked to process and visualise that data and should be involved in discussions around any issues discovered.

---

27 A web template engine enforces the presentation of each page within an application. Each page will have a similar look and feel while the content of each area is different.

Perhaps the most common web analytics technology at the time of writing is Google Analytics, thanks in no small part to it being free (up to a point (Ganguly, 2015)) and it having peer support from a vast user base.

Web analytics represents just one area where we can embrace research, and it produces concrete data we can analyse about factors outside our purview, such as the impact a social media marketing campaign might have on page impressions. There are more research techniques we can employ to justify the decisions we make and persuade our employers and colleagues of their validity, and I would like to spend some time investigating this area next.

Research

John W. Creswell (2008) defines research as 'a process of steps used to collect and analyse information to increase our understanding of a topic or issue' (p. 3). It consists of three fundamental steps:

1. Define the question.

2. Collect data to answer the question.

3. Present the answer.

This research process can be expanded to include other actions (Blankenship, 2010), but generally these are the three main steps.

There are at least four methods of research available to the front-end developer (primary, secondary, generative and evaluative), and these will be detailed further within this section. However, to start we will look at why research can be a vital technique for the front-end developer to learn.

An introduction to research

Let me give you some context as to why research is so vital for front-end developers. A colleague who was not overly well versed in front-end development, being primarily a back-end developer, was asked to develop a system for adding individuals to a table – with all individuals being members of the same family. She asked me for some input on the best process and I, in turn, asked another front-end developer for their opinion. During this second consultation, we disagreed about the best approach, so I decided to carry out some user research to discover the best approach.

Thus a pleasant afternoon was spent working up a couple of prototypes, both coming from the main page which asked the user to enter details about themselves and the members of their family. I used a table for the family members with the user details entered in simple fields such as 'Title', 'Forename', 'Surname' and 'Date of birth'. The same features were required for each family member. They were entered using a modal dialog and displayed in a DataTable enhanced table, where there were also buttons which could be clicked to either remove a family member or edit their details.

My fellow front-end developer said that the best way of getting more details about each family member was to ask the user to enter each specific item one at a time. In our test, we decided that the family members' handedness, eye colour and hair colour would be the most straightforward set of details to obtain, so we created tables for each attribute. The user first created the family members on one page and then they entered the details using multiple modal dialogs, first selecting the family member using a single `select` input and then choosing the eye colour, handedness and hair colour. When an attribute was added for a family member, the modal dialog was closed and the details shown in another table. The details could be removed or edited by clicking on buttons in the row. This method of entering the data meant that each attribute had its table, and the whole page had three separate tables with three different modal dialogs.

My approach was to display each family member within a table, with each attribute being related to a column in the table and each family member represented by a row. While there was no facility to remove a family member, each cell in the column which was not the name of a family member had a button on it which prompted the user to enter details. Clicking on this button called a modal dialog with a simple `select` for the attribute. Once a value had been selected and the modal dismissed, the relevant cell was updated, but the value for the attribute was in the form of a button so that the user could again invoke the modal dialog and either update or remove the attribute (see Figure 3.5).

For the test to be as unbiased as possible, we provided instructions on the first page with the user able to choose the two options afterwards; each had similar instructions, differing only in their implementation. The family members' attributes were base64[28] encoded and added to the URL, so the details were transmitted between the parent page and its two child pages. I then sent out an email to everyone in the company and shared a link to the test on Facebook to get as many people trying both methods as possible.

Once I had uploaded the files to Firebase for hosting (Myers, 2018c), checked everything was working correctly, emailed everyone and then asked people to comment via social media, I returned to my original work to await the results with some quiet satisfaction, as I do love a bit of action research. I did not have to wait long, though, as helpful colleagues started testing as soon as they got the email.

I used Firebase as it offers free hosting for a small number of files. While I could have written the test using a single-page application (SPA) using something like Vue on JSFiddle, I wanted to get it out and gather the data as quickly as possible,

---

28 Though primarily used to encode binary data, base64 can also be used to encode other data. It uses a different number base from decimal to encode data, such that the string 'Hello World' would become 'SGVsbG8gV29ybGQ='. It can be useful when transferring data because it removes spaces without encoding them – for example, encoding 'Hello World' results in 'Hello%20World' using traditional encoding.

Figure 3.5 Single-table approach

Thank you again for taking part in this test, you're very nearly done.

If you can see a table below with 4 people in it (Doctors 08 08 (08/08/0808), 09 09 (09/09/0909), 10 10 (10/10/1010) and 11 11 (11/11/1111)) then you're ready to go. We'd like you to add some details for the family. You (as Dr 08 08) have brown hair, brown eyes and you're left-handed. The rest of your family has these details:

- Dr. 09 09 is really rather odd with silver eyes, white hair and is ambidextrous (I'm not sure I'd trust them TBH).
- Dr. 10 10, perhaps due to being ambilevous, had a rather tragic accident and has no eyes or hair as a result.
- Dr. 11 11 is right-handed and has brown hair and eyes.

If you could provide the details and be mindful about how the process feels to you, perhaps in relation to how the other version felt if you've already entered the data there, then get back to us we'd be really grateful. I'll be sharing this on Facebook so a comment there will suffice but please try entering the data in both ways before commenting.

We appreciate that the scenario is contrived but it's just a made up use case, no data you enter is saved to a server, it's all in the browser - though the initial page does make use of local storage so that the details of the family are maintained between sessions.

Show | 10 > | entries

Search: _____

Family Member	↕ Eye Colour	Hair Colour	Hand Dominance
Dr. 08 08 (08/08/0808)	Brown | Edit Eye Colour	Brown | Edit Hair Colour	Left-handed | Edit Handedness
Dr. 09 09 (09/09/0909)	Silver | Edit Eye Colour	White | Edit Hair Colour	Ambidextrous | Edit Handedness
Dr. 10 10 (10/10/1010)	Add Eye Colour	Add Hair Colour	Ambilevous | Edit Handedness
Dr. 11 11 (11/11/1111)	Brown | Edit Eye Colour	Brown | Edit Hair Colour	Right-handed | Edit Handedness

Showing 1 to 4 of 4 entries

Previous | 1 | Next

Go Back

and at the time I was not overly familiar with SPAs. In reflection, an SPA would have provided a much faster mechanism as, rather than loading three pages' worth of HTML, CSS and JavaScript for each page, one page would have contained all the markup, styling and business logic. Further, I could have taken advantage of a state management pattern[29] such as Vuex, as well as Lazy Loading[30] to ensure that only the relevant data would be within the browser.

In the process of collating the results of the test, I was pleased to note that my idea won out, with 16 out of 18 respondents preferring the single table, one favouring the multiple tables and one not expressing a preference. I had requested feedback on each user's preference and any comments. This mixture of open and closed questions[31] was useful as we wanted to gain a definitive answer regarding the choice of input method as well as to garner further details as to why that option was preferred. Three respondents were concerned about the real-estate of the multiple tables approach and were worried that users might not have the patience to scroll.

Those respondents with experience of front-end development and familiarity with user experience suggested that each method was suited to different scenarios, with all but one choosing the single-table approach. While the details of our example did not replicate the purpose of the original

---

29 A state management pattern is logic which keeps track of the data within an application to perform a function, such as disabling submit buttons unless all required fields are filled in within a form. There are many options available to developers, but many frameworks have their preferred solutions.

30 Lazy Loading addresses the concern mentioned in the text. Rather than there being a need to load multiple single pages, routing allows all the resources required for multiple pages to be loaded at once. Thus, duplicate resources such as HTML (for elements which will not change during the application lifecycle, such as headers and footers) and CSS need load only once. This does mean that the initial load can be larger, though, as the business logic for all pages must be downloaded. One way of addressing this is for the page to automatically download those specific parts of the application only when they are required using Lazy Loading.

31 Open questions are those which cannot be answered by simply saying 'yes' or 'no' but invite a richer response. They can be very useful but difficult to categorise. Closed questions have a pre-determined set of possible answers (such as 'yes' and 'no').

developer's question, the example was analogous regarding the quantity of information being sought.

A nice side-effect of using the single-table method related to the underlying data structure. We were storing the details in JavaScript Object Notation (JSON) and each interaction with the table, and its associated modal dialogs, triggered the DataTable to call its `draw` function, allowing us to update the underlying JSON object. This could even have been used to make AJAX calls to update the data on the server (or Salesforce, in this instance).

Primary research
The above process is an example of primary research, which can also include:

- **Action research:** this type of research came from the social sciences but has a place within front-end development. It involves making changes and then judging the impact of the changes through reflection. This reflection does not need to be limited to you but can include any of the other methods of research.

- **Asking research subjects to engage in an interaction using a prototype:** we have looked at this approach already and noted the difficulties associated with it in terms of the expertise of the subjects.

- **Conducting interviews:** interviews can be held in several different ways, with some occurring face to face and others taking place over the telephone or an online chat system. Interviews are much more personal than other research methods, but this can be one of their downfalls in that any bias on the part of the interviewer may be transferred to the interviewee. They may also produce extraneous data, especially if the interviewer uses open questions.

- **The use of user groups:** user groups are like interviews but engage more users and so can garner results from many individuals at the same time. Again the question of bias must be acknowledged with this type of research.

The chance of bias occurring may be increased by the inclusion of powerful or influential members within the user group.

- **Contextual inquiries:** these are semi-structured interviews carried out while the user is engaged in the subject of the research. In the case of front-end developer research, this means that the user is questioned while they are involved in the process being developed to see if their perception of their journey matches the journey observed. This kind of research can be excellent but it does take time.

- **Diary studies:** these are like contextual inquires but take place over a period of time. For example, a user might be asked to interact with an application for a week and to document their feelings regarding its ease of use over that period once the initial shock of the new has worn off.

All types of primary research collect data directly from subjects, meaning that the data is fresh. In contrast, secondary research (considered next) generally uses distilled information from primary research. All methods are open to bias, though, and they do take significant time to implement.

Secondary research

Answering a question by referring to existing resources (such as academic sources or the writings of experts in the field) and previous research often means that it is possible to avoid duplicating the effort made by someone else and reach an answer quicker. However, it does require some facility with search engines, as we need to understand how to ask our question.

Often secondary research is my first approach to answering a question as it requires the least effort; rather than designing a prototype and thinking about which research methodologies would be most useful to answer my question, I prefer to first see whether the problem already has an answer. This secondary research takes the form of reading books, asking questions in relevant forums such as Stack Exchange (while

Stack Overflow will eventually become a resource you will use daily in your professional life, there are many other forums under its umbrella), and using multiple search engines.

Secondary research can also be useful to support your decisions regarding design choices you make. One area where this is important is forms. There are many different decisions to make regarding forms. For example, sometimes it seems to make logical sense to group inputs next to each other, such as start date and end date for entering a duration – you will doubtless have seen such design choices in practice. However, this is not the best way of entering such data. This justification can be used to defend your decisions to any stakeholder who might question them.

Generative research
Generative, sometimes known as exploratory, research overlaps with primary research significantly, as it involves gaining a deeper understanding of the question being asked and the essential reason for its posing. It consists of looking at the world around you for opportunities to improve and innovate, but it does run the risk of creating something that is never used as it was never required.

For instance, as a front-end developer you might be tasked with improving interaction in a specific area of an application. Primary research in the form of interviews might reveal complaints from a few users about one particular mechanism, that of adding tasks to a system. A modal dialog is displayed upon clicking a button and the details of the task are entered within a form, which is submitted to the server for storage. Some of the users note that they often have to enter multiple tasks at one time and have to repeatedly open the modal by clicking on the button. In this scenario, you might decide to add an option at the end of the modal dialog which allows the creation of a new task without waiting for the last to be saved, thus eliminating a single keypress to invoke another dialog. This could be done either by adding a checkbox at the end of the form with the label 'Add another task' or by adding a button next to the 'Save' option with the text 'Save and add another'. While this might not seem like a massive saving for users, it will be noticed and might lead users to have small moments of delight. This possibility can be confirmed via further interviews.

This is an example of generative research, because you were tasked with improving a general area but you did not know what you would do to improve it until you saw the results of interviews. You then decided to add the option to add another task. The example does make use of primary research as well. Janelle Estes (2020) of User Testing has written about the ways that information can be gathered for generative research as well as the differences between generative research and the next type of research we will examine: evaluative research.

Evaluative research

Evaluative research helps us to understand how our users think while interacting with an application and provides some feedback on the solution developed as a result of the initial primary research. For example, using the family example above, once the decision had been taken on which approach to take to gather the required information from users (either a single table or multiple tables), then the users would be asked for their feelings about the finished application. This kind of feedback can be instrumental in the realm of front-end development as it allows us to gather evidence to justify our decisions and can inform future work.

As an aside, in our example, we asked our users for feedback at the end of the process of completing the task. This is known as a 'summative assessment'. If we had asked our users for their thoughts while they were working through the task, then we would have been employing 'formative assessments'. Both formative and summative assessments can be carried out, and they might give further insights, such as any challenges that users encounter while engaged in the task.[32] Both formative

---

[32] Such challenges can also be called 'transitive challenges', and in this instance they might not be picked up at the end of the process. If someone finds it difficult to interact with a process but is pleased at the conclusion, then often the challenges are forgotten as a result of the relief of completing the process.

and summative assessments can be used in primary and evaluative research.

Further thoughts on research

This section has only touched on a few areas of research, but this is a vast area and it can be extremely important for front-end developers. I encourage you to investigate further and to engage in research. To an extent, we are all involved in research all the time, and the work we produce throughout our career serves as generative research to inform our future practice. Asking a question is good; understanding your need to ask the question is even better and will undoubtedly have an impact on the solution you reach.

You may well have come across the term 'A/B testing'. If you have enough time at your disposal, you might want to use this method of experimentation to find the best possible solution. In A/B testing, subjects are assigned to one of two options or approaches (A or B) randomly, so as to enable the front-end developer to judge which is the most successful approach. A/B testing can even be widened to use more than two approaches; this is known as 'multivariate testing'. Despite the time associated with A/B testing and the fiddly nature of deploying solutions with two different approaches, it is an advantageous way of judging the impact of changes.

However you approach your research activity, you must engage in some sort of research. It gives you a greater facility to make the user comfortable with your software and fulfil your role as a front-end developer to the best of your ability.

Special care should be taken to ensure research is ethical. Consent needs to be obtained in all research using human participants and not assumed once the study has started. Participants must also be able to leave the study whenever they desire. Any sensitive data should be handled sympathetically and kept confidentially. Informing participants why they are engaged in the research is also vital (Mortensen, 2018).

> I would suggest reading Ditte Mortensen's article 'Conducting Ethical User Research' to gain a greater understanding of ethical research considerations (Mortensen, 2018).

Research is not the only area where the front-end developer must consider ethics; we will examine this area further at the end of this chapter.

Data

We have looked at ways of displaying data in tables and other visualisations but have spent very little time looking at ways of storing data. In this section we will look at JavaScript Object Notation (JSON) and also touch on databases. While you might not be tasked with working directly with a database, you will doubtless be asked to display data retrieved from one, so it is worth having an understanding of the underlying technology.

JSON

JSON can be used similarly to XML in that it is a data-interchange format that uses human-readable text to transmit data objects. Like the all-encompassing structure of XML, each JSON object is enclosed within a single pair of curly brackets (also known as braces). JSON is an unordered set of name–value pairs. Where things get interesting, though, is that the value can be any native JavaScript data, including JSON itself, meaning that we can have an object which holds an array of family member objects and those family member objects can have, for example, titles, forenames, surnames, dates of birth, eye colour, hair colour and handedness name–value pairs.

Despite it coming from JavaScript, many other languages are also able to generate and parse JSON. For example, if we were to use XML, we would shrink it down by using many more attributes rather than elements to reach a similar level of compression to that of JSON, meaning that in the example of the family data-gathering research we looked at earlier, the JSON would come in at 1,034 characters, the XML at 1,124, and the XML (using attributes rather than elements) at 748. Removing the speech marks around the name in JSON name–value pairs seems to be a more and more popular way of writing JSON, but even doing that in the example of the family we discussed earlier would only make the character count 976. Why this is important is all down to speed: the fewer characters transmitted, the better in terms of the responsiveness of the application.

Despite the size differences in our example, Josh Wyse (2014) suggests that JSON is a clear winner over XML, saying that XML uses more words than is necessary and XML parsing is cumbersome because of the repetitive nature of the format. This qualification is sometimes correct, but we have been parsing an XML-like format since the introduction of HTML – the formats are very similar – and all modern browsers have a built-in XML parser that can convert text into an XML DOM which can then be interrogated. The interrogation of the resulting XML DOM can be clunky, though.

Consider the following HTML:

```
<div id="member">
    <p id="title"></p>
    <p id="forename"></p>
    <p id="surname"></p>
    <p id="dateOfBirth"></p>
    <p id="hairColour"></p>
    <p id="eyeColour"></p>
    <p id="handedness"></p>
</div>
```

Following is how we would populate it with a family member from XML using attributes:

```
const familyXML = `
  <family>
    <member
```

```
      title="Dr"
      forename="08"
      surname="08"
      dateOfBirth="08/08/0808"
      hairColour="brown"
      eyeColour="brown"
      handedness="left"/>
  </family>
`;

const parser = new DOMParser();
const xmlDoc = parser
  .parseFromString(
    familyXML,
    "text/xml"
  );
const member = xmlDoc
  .getElementsByTagName("member")[0];
for (let i in member.attributes) {
  const attr = member.attributes[i];
  let el = document
    .getElementById(attr.name);
  if (el) {
    el.innerHTML =
      `${attr.name}: ${attr.value}`;
  }
}
```

When we use JSON, though, this is the equivalent JavaScript:

```
const familyJSON = {
  "family": [
    {
      "title": "Dr",
      "forename": "08",
      "surname": "08",
      "dateOfBirth": "08/08/0808",
      "hairColour": "brown",
      "eyeColour": "brown",
      "handedness": "left"
    }
```

```
  ]
};
const member = familyJSON.family[0];
for (const i in member) {
  document.getElementById(i).innerHTML =
    `${i}: ${member[i]}`;
}
```

To get the member from the XML, we needed to invoke a DOMParser (W3Schools, 2020e) and then search it for the correct family member. Once we have the right family member, we then need to fetch its attributes and iterate[33] over them to update the HTML. In the JSON example, we are lucky that families are small in comparison to other potential data sets. Care must be taken when looking through JSON as it is unordered, so it is always important to properly check that what you get is what you wanted. Iterating over the object (which did not require any extra parsing) is trivial using more modern JavaScript (Mozilla, 2020e) – so insignificant that I did not feel the need to check the intermediate **attr** variable and instead used the **i** variable.

This ease of use is at the heart of Wyse's (2014) assertion that JSON is the preferred format because instead of having to navigate the tree that XML represents, we alternatively browse a map. While the map can be limiting (it is a truism to say that the map is not the territory (Lesswrongwiki, 2012)), Wyse goes on to suggest that limiting the developer is not a bad thing because it makes the code simpler, predictable and easier to read. That is certainly borne out by the code examples above. Further, there are fewer, if any, intermediary steps required for a JSON object to be converted into a native code object as it aligns itself to object-oriented programming concepts.

Both XML and JSON have their place, but more and more APIs seem to be moving towards the JSON format if they are not already using it. Even the popular MySQL relational database management system (RDBMS) now supports JSON natively,

---

33 In computer programming, 'iteration' is the act of repeating a set of actions. In the example above, we would repeatedly examine each family member until we reach the end.

allowing it to be interrogated (though the syntax is a little obtuse – to my eyes at least).

I mentioned SQL and NoSQL when we looked at Agile methodologies earlier in this chapter, and I have just mentioned RDBMS, so let's look at these in greater detail next.

Relational databases and SQL

A database is an organised collection of data. Like most of the subjects we have covered thus far, databases have evolved, but mostly they stem from the 1970s and the work of Dr Edgar F. Codd (1970), who proposed the relational modal. It was not until computer hardware became sufficiently robust, in the 1980s, that relational databases were widely adopted.

Before Codd did his work, databases used either the hierarchical or network models. In the former, the relationships between entities form a tree-like structure that, while simple, is inflexible, with each link confined to a one-to-many relationship. As an approach, databases gained further appreciation with the rise of XML – another tree-like structure – in the late 1990s. This led to the XML database, a type of NoSQL database (more of which later in this section).

Network-based databases, on the other hand, do not limit the relationships between entities to the one-to-many kind. Instead, they are far more flexible regarding links, with any entity able to have multiple parent and child entities.

The distinction between the two is interesting in that in hierarchical models, an entity can have a single parent, while in a network model, an object can have multiple parents. Looking at it another way, both use one-to-many relationships, but network models are less picky about which the parent is, and which the child.

A relational database must be traversed if it is to be queried, and the relationships between entities must be known. The relational model is currently supreme among databases, and, at its heart, it is all about storing like with like. In the data for the family example introduced earlier in this chapter, we have a table for individuals with a finite number of columns, each associated with a specific attribute of the family member, such as `title`, `forename`, `surname`, `dateOfBirth`, `hairColour`, `eyeColour` and `handedness`. We can present this using a table, as shown in Table 3.1.

Each column holds a specific type of data, and we tell the database what that is when we create it. Our data is contrived, but most columns would be of a string type, except for `dateOfBirth`, which would be of a date type.

What would happen, though, if we needed to store the addresses or the phone numbers of the family members? We could add further columns to the table such that there would be columns for each element of the address and the phone numbers, but we would be repeating ourselves as multiple people would have the same address. And suppose the family moved or the address was entered incorrectly for one member of the family – or, heaven forfend, a family member had multiple phone numbers?

Our data starts to get complicated when there begins to be a need for 'normalisation', a term first introduced by Codd (1970). Normalisation seeks to ensure that data is clean and reduces redundancy so that the same data is not held in more than one place.

It is likely that you will have to think about normalisation during your career, but perhaps not so much as you embark on your career. It is an important subject and something worth knowing about even if you do not use it professionally. Once it gets into your thinking, it is pervasive. I remember learning about it at college and thinking that it was just about the best thing ever. It just seemed such a neat and tidy way of organising data.

Table 3.1 How the family members could be stored in a database

title	forename	surname	dateOfBirth	hairColour	eyeColour	handedness
Dr	08	08	08/08/0808	brown	brown	left
Dr	09	09	09/09/0909	white	silver	ambidextrous
Dr	10	10	10/10/1010			ambilevous
Dr	11	11	11/11/1111	brown	brown	right

To interact with a relational database, we use Structured Query Language (SQL). There are many different dialects of SQL. As a language, it is not all that impenetrable as it uses English words which do what they suggest, such as **select**, **update**, **delete** and **insert**.

One thing that front-end developers need to be aware of is SQL injection attacks. In an SQL injection attack, a user replaces the data we are expecting with an SQL command. So, instead of getting a user's first name, we might get, and subsequently pass to the back-end of our application, an SQL command which destroys our database. These attacks are why validation in front-end forms must always be supplemented by back-end validation. Another way of guarding against SQL injection, and a way of evening the field between different SQL dialects, is to use database abstraction layers[34] or other language-specific interfaces and frameworks.

My favourite framework for interacting with MySQL is PHP's Medoo (Lai, 2018), but that is primarily because a lot of my personal development experience has involved using the Linux, Apache, MySQL and PHP (LAMP) stack to create applications. Many of my current colleagues swear by Microsoft's Language Integrated Query (LINQ) framework, and more recently Facebook's GraphQL has gained popularity, with some hailing it as a replacement for Representational State Transfer (REST).[35]

REST was developed to correspond with the Hypertext Transfer Protocol (HTTP), the foundation of data communication for the World Wide Web. You will most

---

[34] A database abstraction layer provides an interface between a computer program and a database. Traditionally, different databases accept slightly different commands. The database abstraction layer provides an identical interface without the developer needing to learn a different database dialect.

[35] MDN Web Docs has a concise introduction to REST (see Mozilla, 2019h).

often come across it when working with simple forms, when data can be sent to the back-end using the GET, POST, PUT, DELETE or PATCH methods. Being asked to describe REST is a favourite interview question, so it is worthwhile spending time familiarising yourself with the concept.

REST is primarily an architectural concept for decoupling an API from the client, whereas GraphQL is a query language, a specification and a collection of tools. Further information can be found in the article 'GraphQL vs REST: Overview' (Sturgeon, 2017).

We have looked at relational databases, the ways of structuring data within them and how to interact with the data within them. But there is an alternative called NoSQL.

NoSQL

NoSQL as a term dates to the opening years of the 21st century and originally came from a relational database which did not expose a standard SQL interface.

The creator of that database, Carlo Strozzi, suggested that the term 'NoSQL' should not be used. Instead, he suggested using the word 'NoREL' to describe databases which are not relational. Despite this suggestion, the name 'NoSQL' has become the *de facto* umbrella term for such databases.

NoSQL databases are difficult to classify as they can fall under different categories, but they generally belong to one of four basic types: key-value stores, document databases, wide-column stores and graph databases (I'm Programmer, 2020). What this means is that we can store the JSON representation of the family we had before in a NoSQL database and not worry about Dr 11 having multiple phone numbers.

Going into further detail about NoSQL databases without a specific context in mind would be something of a fool's errand as, depending on your requirements and circumstances, you have multiple options available to you. I would therefore encourage you to do your own research into your specific use case.

NoSQL databases are cheaper to provision than relational databases as, when a relational database needs to be scaled up in size, it either requires more powerful hardware or must be distributed among multiple servers, and the handling of tables across different servers can be difficult. Some NoSQL databases are designed to be scalable from the outset, and the complexity associated with scaling is reduced. This focus on scalability means that they are also suited to utilising cheaper hardware. This use of more affordable equipment further reduces their cost, especially as some relational databases charge significant amounts for licences.

A further advantage of NoSQL databases is that the data is not structured. If the business requirements change regarding the data required, a traditional database might need to be re-architected to conform with the three normal forms of normalisation. In contrast, in a NoSQL database, it is possible to add new information to records on the fly.

The unstructured nature of the data has negatives too, though. Many developers spend years training their minds to understand normalisation and now do it almost subconsciously, with the result that they are very familiar with the SQL **JOIN**.[36] NoSQL systems do sometimes lead to the issues normalisation seeks to address, with data being replicated unnecessarily.

TESTING

Testing will undoubtedly make up at least a small part of any interview you have for the role of front-end developer, so it is

---

[36] A JOIN clause within SQL is used to combine rows from two or more tables based on the related column between them.

worthwhile spending time writing and implementing tests in even the most trivial examples of your code. We will take a brief look at this subject now, but do ensure that any code you submit as a part of the interview process has at least some basic tests.

Testing within front-end development can be split into three main areas: end-to-end testing, integration testing and unit testing. We will look at each in turn.

End-to-end testing

End-to-end (E2E) testing is also known as user interface (UI) testing, and this is where a good QA team member is worth their weight in gold, as they take the stress out of testing every aspect of the application when changes are made. This kind of testing is carried out to ensure that changes have not broken any part of the application (these are sometimes referred to as 'breaking changes'). It is possible to automate some or all parts of E2E testing, using something like Selenium (https://selenium.dev), which can be scripted to interact with a browser window and await responses to actions before continuing. With the introduction of headless browsers,[37] this process has been made much faster. It may well be that, if you have a QA person within your team, they will employ such automated testing.

Integration testing

Also known as functional or snapshot testing, this involves testing the interactions between different elements of your application, such as communication between various UI components or between UI components and the back-end of the application. It might even involve testing the UI component

---

[37] A headless browser is a browser without a graphical user interface. The HTML and other elements exist but are not displayed so there is far less of an overhead in terms of testing the application as the headless browser can be controlled via a script.

against something like the `localStorage` property[38] or cookies.[39]

Unit testing

Unit testing involves testing components, methods or functions in isolation. Unit testing is by far the easiest way of testing and can be automated quickly and simply using a wealth of testing frameworks, such as Jest (https://jestjs.io).[40] At its most basic, a testing script compares the result of a function with the expected result. Following is an example of a simple Jest test to check that a function which adds two numbers works as expected:

```
const sum = (a, b) => a + b;

test('adds 1 + 2 to equal 3', () => {
    expect(sum(1, 2)).toBe(3);
});
```

Testing overview

While E2E, integration and unit testing make up the testing pyramid (see Figure 3.6), there are other tests you need to be aware of, such as testing CSS[41] and page-speed testing.

There is some discussion about whether testing should be approached from the top of the pyramid or the bottom, with

---

38 Data which is stored within the browser and is persistent between sessions so that data stored can be accessed by the application the next time it is run. It is a relatively new technique and used to be limited to cookies.

39 The first type of local storage, cookies are stored in small text files and can be read by the application. They are often added to any requests made by the application to the back-end.

40 Described by its makers as a 'Delightful JavaScript Testing Framework', it was developed by Facebook and is primarily used for testing React applications, but it can test all JavaScript.

41 CSS testing is introduced very well by Chris Coyier in the article 'Automatic CSS Testing' (Coyier, 2015).

Figure 3.6 The testing pyramid

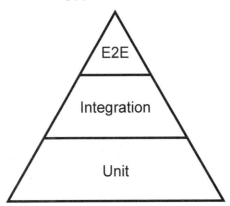

Stefano Magni (2019) arguing that rather than picking the low-hanging fruit by working from the bottom up, approaching testing from the top down might mean that you will avoid having to write integration and unit tests as you already know that the application is working. If an E2E test fails, though, the other tests are valuable in terms of pinpointing the cause of the failure.

Along with others (e.g. Yerburgh, 2017), Magni also points out that the pyramid could be reversed in terms of time and effort required, with unit testing being easy and fast, integration testing being less easy and slightly slower, and end-to-end testing taking by far the most time and effort.

Speed testing[42] is essential and can often be picked up during integration testing as the interactions between different parts of the application may highlight issues if there is a significant delay.

---

[42] Google provides a tool, called PageSpeed Insights, which can help with some initial testing (https://developers.google.com/speed/pagespeed/insights).

ETHICS

An additional benefit of developing the empathy I suggested earlier in this book (see Chapter 2) would hopefully be an enhanced sense of ethics. It might not be obvious why ethics is essential to front-end development, but it plays a massive part in what you will be doing.

We have an ethical responsibility to both our employers and our users to produce a quality solution, but there can be conflict within that responsibility. We will have honed and developed expertise in providing solutions to our users, but our employers may well choose to ignore our suggestions and ask us to create solutions which act against a subset of our potential users. For example, if we know that a colour scheme will make an application illegible to a subset of our users but our employer insists upon it, what should we do? We can point out that 1 in 20 Caucasian males are colour blind (Bailey, 2018) and that the business would thus run the risk of alienating 5% of its male market, but, given a directive to use the colour scheme, can we refuse?

Judging where your ethical concerns direct you to step away from a role can be difficult.

Morten Rand-Hendriksen (2018) believes that ethics should be a core component of web design and computer science in general, primarily because what we do has such a direct impact on our users. It can help significantly to personalise users by imagining someone close to you yet technically less adept using the application you are enhancing. After all, we hope that many users will use our work, so our audience could be huge! Even the smallest decisions we make have the potential to impact a significant portion of the population, so it is vital that we make the best choices we can.

The BCS Code of Conduct

One starting point for developing your ethical position is the BCS Code of Conduct (BCS – The Chartered Institute for IT, 2015).

Public interest

Of particular relevance to front-end developers is the section on public interest, which states that you shall:

a. have due regard for public health, privacy, security and wellbeing of others and the environment;

b. have due regard for the legitimate rights of Third Parties (the term 'Third Parties' includes any person or organisation that might be affected by your activities in your professional capacity, irrespective of whether they are directly aware or involved in those activities);

c. conduct your professional activities without discrimination on the grounds of sex, sexual orientation, marital status, nationality, colour, race, ethnic origin, religion, age or disability, or of any other condition or requirement;

d. promote equal access to the benefits of IT and seek to promote the inclusion of all sectors in society wherever opportunities arise.

As a springboard for developing your distinct ethical standpoint, you cannot ask for a better base, but do not merely follow these four rules blindly. Instead, examine them and try to put yourself, or those you care about, in the frame.

I like that BCS chooses to put 'public interest' above 'professional competence and integrity', 'duty to relevant authority' and 'duty to the profession' in its Code of Conduct, because public interest is the most crucial aspect of the work we do. The other areas should not be ignored, however.

Kostya Stepanov (2017) has written about his ethical standpoint. In not taking on a contract from a rival of an existing client, which cost him and his company $100,000, he took a laudable ethical stand. Thankfully his morals did not harm him in the long run, as you will see from reading the article, but there will be situations where acting ethically will have a harmful effect. What you choose to do in such cases is up to you, but I know from my own experience that avoiding feelings of guilt is almost as satisfying as altruism.

Professional competence and integrity
In terms of professional competence and integrity, again BCS has you covered with its seven guidelines. The Code states that you shall, as a member of BCS (although this advice applies equally to the IT profession at large, regardless of whether you are a member of BCS):

a. only undertake to do work or provide a service that is within your professional competence;

b. NOT claim any level of competence that you do not possess;

c. develop your professional knowledge, skills and competence on a continuing basis, maintaining awareness of technological developments, procedures, and standards that are relevant to your field;

d. ensure that you have the knowledge and understanding of Legislation (the term 'Legislation' means any applicable laws, statutes and regulations) and that you comply with such Legislation, in carrying out your professional responsibilities;

e. respect and value alternative viewpoints and, seek, accept and offer honest criticisms of work;

f. avoid injuring others, their property, reputation, or employment by false or malicious or negligent action or inaction;

g. reject and will not make any offer of bribery or unethical inducement.

Regarding only undertaking to do work or provide a service that is within your professional competence, learning by doing can be useful. However, do appreciate that sometimes it is appropriate to suggest a certain piece of work is carried out by someone else in the team if they are more skilled in the area and thus will be capable of doing the task much faster. Alternatively, you can ask colleagues for help to both up-skill yourself and ensure the work is completed promptly.

Duty to relevant authority

The next section of the Code deals with our duty to our relevant authority, with 'relevant authority' defined as most usually our employer or client. It states that you shall:

a. carry out your professional responsibilities with due care and diligence in accordance with the Relevant Authority's requirements whilst exercising your professional judgement at all times;

b. seek to avoid any situation that may give rise to a conflict of interest between you and your Relevant Authority;

c. accept professional responsibility for your work and for the work of colleagues who are defined in a given context as working under your supervision;

d. NOT disclose or authorise to be disclosed, or use for personal gain or to benefit a third party, confidential information except with the permission of your Relevant Authority, or as required by Legislation;

e. NOT misrepresent or withhold information on the performance of products, systems or services (unless lawfully bound by a duty of confidentiality not to disclose such information), or take advantage of the lack of relevant knowledge or inexperience of others.

These are all quite straightforward instructions, and the first is something we should always strive to achieve. Taking pride in one's work seems a quite straightforward ideal and is certainly something I hope I have illustrated in this book, even if it only relates to ensuring that your code is indented correctly.

One area not expressly covered by the Code of Conduct is that of employers clawing back training costs. Many employers now ask for repayment if you leave soon after completing a course or training. For instance, PRINCE2 training costs more than £1,000 and involves a significant investment of time both from yourself and your employer. Any time you need to take off to study can become quite expensive for your employer too. This investment of time and money means that your employer might be able to pursue more lucrative contracts, but it also makes you significantly more employable. Would it be fair to leave directly after finishing the course and getting your certificate? I would suggest that you should spend some time justifying your employer's investment by continuing to work for them for a while. However, if you decide to leave, be aware that an employer can only ask you to repay training costs if it has previously been agreed that you will do so (Citizens Advice, 2018). Many contracts now include such a provision, so please do check.

Duty to the profession
The final section of the Code details your duty to the profession, saying that you shall:

a. accept your personal duty to uphold the reputation of the profession and not take any action which could bring the profession into disrepute;

b. seek to improve professional standards through participation in their development, use and enforcement;

c. uphold the reputation and good standing of BCS, the Chartered Institute for IT;

d. act with integrity and respect in your professional relationships with all members of BCS and with members of other professions with whom you work in a professional capacity;

e. notify BCS if convicted of a criminal offence or upon becoming bankrupt or disqualified as a Company Director and in each case give details of the relevant jurisdiction;

f. encourage and support fellow members in their professional development.

On the sixth point, I would hope that encouraging others to develop professionally will eventually lead them to join BCS. By acting as a positive example to others, you will foster in them an appreciation of the professionalism of the IT industry and the professional framework offered by BCS.

SUMMARY

We have covered a considerable number of subjects in this chapter, all of which are worthy of far, far greater exploration. By a long way, the most critical technologies you need to be comfortable with are HTML, CSS and JavaScript – you will likely be able to pick the others up along the way. The quantity of information available to you when it comes to learning these methods and techniques is almost limitless, and your employer will doubtless have preferred sources of such learning. Ask your employer and your friends and colleagues about relevant resources and how they learnt, and you should be well set.

4 A DAY IN THE LIFE OF A FRONT-END DEVELOPER

The preceding chapters looked at the tools, methods and techniques employed by front-end developers. However, we are yet to discuss how these are used in day-to-day employment. This chapter therefore looks at what a front-end developer might expect to do in a day.

There is no typical day in the life of any developer, let alone a front-end developer. I have therefore included a bit of everything in this day to illustrate all the possibilities of the job, so this is going to seem like a very, very full day. Please do not think that I am always this busy all day and please do not let this put you off joining the profession. On an average day, I would likely spend a bit of time on one or two features of the discipline, but in far greater depth.

You will notice that I break my day up into multiple short chunks. These breaks are deliberate; taking mini-breaks improves focus and concentration and is better for your body as well, allowing you the chance to move around.

I work exclusively from home in my current role and have done so for the past couple of years, but the structure of my day has not changed much since I began to work from home, except that I now no longer need to commute for a couple of hours each day.

MORNING

08:00–09:30

I generally start my day by checking any work-related emails that came in during the evening and night.

> I know that some people check their emails when they are away from work, but I caution against that. I find that if I do check my work emails, then I do not really relax but instead find myself preparing for the coming day when I should be relaxing.

After checking emails, I either pick up the tasks I have been asked to address via email or continue with the jobs I was engaged upon when I downed tools the previous day. I sometimes deliberately leave something in progress so that my subconscious can have a crack at it during the night.

I also spend some time looking over pertinent front-end-specific items via Feedly and click through to read the full article when they are relevant to me. I only look at them in greater depth when I need to take a break later in the day. These professional 'distractions' keep me updated, help me generate new ideas and, occasionally, help me find a solution to any current frustrations.

09:30–09:45

At 09:30 my colleagues and I have our stand-up. Stand-ups are a mainstay of Agile, which I discussed in Chapter 3. It is the *de facto* approach to development at the time of writing, and you will more than likely work within its dictates if you have not already done so.

> I say that Agile is a standard within development, but it appears that it is reaching into other areas of human endeavour. Most recently, I heard from a friend in nursing that what were once called 'handovers' are now known as stand-ups.

Our stand-up is online, and we are all usually sitting down and talking over Skype. It lasts no more than 15 minutes and involves us each discussing what we did over the previous day as well as outlining what we plan to do over the coming day. It is also an opportunity to briefly discuss any development problems or issues that we're facing and seek help from other members of the team. It is important to note, though, that issues are not discussed in length but introduced and then discussed further in a follow-up conversation with only the relevant members of the team attending and offering help or suggestions.

At this stand-up, I note that I have resolved a couple of issues which were raised during our user acceptance testing[1] and also found and resolved a bug that was only evident in Internet Explorer 11 (I needed to replace an ES6 arrow function with a regular JavaScript function which had been written by another developer). I also detail what I plan to do during the rest of the day.

09:45–11:00

I have been asked to look at a form we have been working on for a client. It is a long and complicated form and requires the user to upload several pieces of evidence before it can be submitted. There has recently been an issue with the form,

---

[1] User acceptance testing (UAT) is carried out to confirm that the application matches the required specification. Our UAT is carried out by a team internal to the business but separate from the development team, so perhaps it should not be classified as UAT, except that the business also uses our product in its day-to-day operation. UAT is a feature of Agile.

with users being unable to progress despite providing an answer to a required question, so I have been asked to correct the problem. This issue highlights the importance of thorough testing before the release of new code – had the developer who changed the validation on the form tested it themselves, they would have seen the issue. It also highlights the importance of understanding the business case for the requirement of the information as the client had changed their mind about the importance of collecting something which previously had not been required.

After relaxing the validation on the form to allow users to progress, I take a break to stretch my legs and make a pot of coffee to drink during the next hour or so.

11:00–11:30

At 11:00 we have a regular developer meeting to go over any issues raised in the stand-up, to look at possible solutions to blockers and impediments, and sometimes to show off.

Taking pride in your work is admirable. Although we generally frown on showing off, displaying something that you have just accomplished is essential.

You are hopefully being paid significant amounts of money for your labours, and it is crucial that not only your co-workers but also the stakeholders among your employers can see your worth. Not only will that help them to justify paying you but it will also prompt them to think in greater depth about what they want from you. If you can provide evidence to show that you can take an idea and make it work elegantly, then they will be far more likely to think of ways in which you can stretch your creativity in the future. Being challenged in this way will improve your engagement in your work and prompt more significant learning and understanding.

As part of the meeting, there is a question about why we have opted to use a flexbox layout (see the relevant section in Chapter 3) on a project. I came to this particular project after many of the significant design decisions had already been made, so I am more than a little interested in the rationale for this choice as well. It seems as though there was a requirement for elements to align within a container – no matter the width of the device used by the user; each part was a fixed width but on wider screens there needed to be a gap between items, whereas on narrower devices the elements needed to wrap appropriately. In this instance, the items were dashboard widgets, and their height is fixed to a multiple of a base unit. Thus the wrapping could get complicated. One possible solution to the issue would be to use a masonry layout where variable-sized blocks of content are pieced together into a whole. We decide to research how to implement a masonry layout during the next sprint.

11:30–12:00

One of my tasks today is to try to figure out why a table is not displaying correctly. We are using DataTables to enhance a table, but for some reason the first row is not displaying correctly. I fix the table in question by putting back the **thead** element and its child **tr** and children **th** items that an over-zealous fellow developer had removed.

I consider the effect the developer was trying to achieve by styling the first row of the table in the way they did but instead style the elements in CSS using the **vw** measurement unit. They have used DataTables and styling the row in the way they did not only broke DataTables but also cut the ordering functionality, as DataTables would have considered the row as a row which should be ordered.

The **vw** measurement unit was introduced in CSS3 and is widely supported (Deveria, n.d.-b). It is an interesting unit of measurement, with 1vw representing 1% of the viewport width. I have been using it extensively of late to ensure that **thead** text is understandable on smaller screens.

LUNCH

By my reckoning, I have been working for something between three and three and a half hours nearly solidly, so I need a break. I have a busy remainder of the day ahead, so I go off to the gym and shops to get something to eat. I then walk the dog on my return.

AFTERNOON

14:00–14:30

I am looking forward to the next tranche of work, which is tweaking some images for inclusion in the current project so that they fit within the page and will continue to do so regardless of the resolution of the user's device. I decide to use a raster image in this context as the image is a photograph.

I feel justified using a JPEG, but I make sure I reduce the quality and thus the size of the image to not cause too many issues for those users with a slower internet connection.

14:30–15:00

I finish writing a report on the results of some user research I carried out a little while ago. I email this research to the internal product owners, being careful to include all relevant parties and include anonymised evidence to support my conclusion that using a single table to collect data would be better than using multiple tables.

15:00–16:00

A quick check of the shared calendar reminds me it is nearly time for our sprint retrospective.

Each team will be different, but in my current team there is a front-end developer (me) and there are at least three other developers who are classed – in our team at least – as full-stack developers. Additionally, there is our Scrum master, our software architect, our designer, a representative from our product owners and a smattering of representatives from quality assurance (QA).

A retrospective is held at the end of an Agile sprint to reflect on what went well and what could be improved for the next sprint. We look at how many tasks we have finished and what is remaining, and we also note that communication has again been key in accomplishing our goals, with QAs particularly praised for seeking clarification regarding testing the work we undertook. There are few stories left to be classified as done[2] and these are carried over into the next sprint.

16:00–17:00

Our retrospective is recorded on an Ideaboardz (https://ideaboardz.com). I look forward to my day's work tomorrow. I know that there are some things that I will have to research and plan this evening so that I am prepared for tomorrow morning's sprint planning meeting, where we will define and specify the work we will be doing in the next sprint. I know, for instance, that I will be spending some time displaying data to users – data which has been supplied to me about a process in the application in JSON format.

---

2   In Agile development, 'done' should really mean 'DONE!' (Waters, 2007).

5   CAREER PROGRESSION

The preceding chapters examined the critical technologies required for front-end development as well as some of the other tools and methodologies you might be expected to use in your career. Let's now look at the profession itself in a little more detail.

BECOMING A FRONT-END DEVELOPER

I know self-taught front-end developers as well as those who have entered the business after completing a PhD (though not necessarily in a sphere closely aligned to computer science). We have seen that the primary personal attributes required are empathy and curiosity – but these are requirements of most, if not all, professions, so what sets front-end developers apart? Knowledge of the tools, methods and techniques we have looked at thus far in this book will stand you in good stead, and a willingness to continue your professional development will make you stand out to your colleagues as well as to potential employers.

In my first role in front-end development, the people I worked with, without exception, were educated to at least degree level. Some had a degree in a sphere closely aligned with computer science, if not actually in computer science. Each of us had a degree, though, as this was thought to be the appropriate indicator that we were suitable for a development role at that point in the progression of the profession. More recently, however, it has become increasingly likely for front-end developers to be self-taught or even to have undergone training in a bootcamp (more on this below). These individuals are still in the minority, but their number is growing.

Employers, particularly smaller companies (Thayer, 2018), are now often less interested than they used to be in candidates who have studied for a generalist computer science degree. They now often prefer applicants with more practical and modern knowledge, those who have perhaps had experience of problem-solving within teams, and those who have dedicated time and resources to seeking specific expertise in a development sphere.

With growing dissatisfaction with university education among both students and employers, there has arisen a specific industry, that of the coding bootcamp. A bootcamp is a training program specifically designed to hone those skills most in demand by employers. Often the most theoretical aspects of a topic are ignored over imparting the skills needed to solve problems likely to confront students in the workplace. It might be worthwhile for traditionally university-educated developers to take a bootcamp or two on specific subjects to add depth to their knowledge.

The knowledge that bootcamps impart can be considerable, but some leave something to be desired. So, if you want to learn front-end development via a bootcamp, I would suggest reading reviews before parting with your cash. Taking several bootcamps and gaining greater depth of understanding is likely to be cheaper in the long run than a university degree, but bear in mind that it does not take into account the other benefits of university education, such as gaining a broader understanding of the subject.

Kyle Thayer (2017) has spent some time researching coding bootcamps. He cautions people who are considering this option that the process of learning the trade and changing careers is likely to take a year. Further, he suggests learning as much as possible before the coding bootcamp and being shrewd when looking at their reported success rates.

Bootcamps might also fulfil the promise of universal education in that, at least in the USA, they attract a higher proportion of women and ethnic minorities than universities. WhatsTheHost.com has a brilliant infographic from which I gleaned this information; it also details other differences between coding bootcamps and a computer science degree (WhatsTheHost Team, 2019).

Having a broad understanding of a field means that you are not merely skilled in one aspect of it but can instead use your knowledge more widely.

I mentioned above that I know self-taught developers. I have an appreciation for the time and effort required to learn in this way, as I have tried it. After spending months and months attempting to teach myself, getting lost in different forms of learning and becoming confused by the plethora of resources available, I chose a part-time conversion MSc, and that suited me far better.

For those who are not beginners, there are a wealth of – possibly far too many – resources available. One of my friends found their way into the profession through engaging with Daniel Shiffman's Coding Train (https://thecodingtrain.com). While Shiffman is an academic, his YouTube videos are an engaging way of learning. They and my friend's further reading and experimentation, including developing applications for friends and family,

> meant that they were eminently qualified for a role in
> the business where we both worked. Again, curiosity was
> vital to their success – that and having a defined goal for
> each area of exploration.

There seems to be no better way of engaging in self-teaching than having a set goal for your scholarship. This appears to be a critical difference between self-learning and bootcamps: whereas bootcamps teach techniques and use example applications, developing an application is an excellent way of picking up techniques as it forces you to experiment and research. A measure of pride is also advantageous here as well – if the application is going to be used by those who are close to you, then you want their experience to be seamless and the application to be flawless. Users should also be less reticent about offering suggestions or criticism.

PROGRESSING AS A FRONT-END DEVELOPER

There are many options for you to develop your skills as you progress as a front-end developer. I have previously touched on the importance of curiosity, and that will be an essential resource in your progression. A desire to keep on learning new techniques and technologies will stand you in good stead, as will a willingness to prove those hard-earned skills with professional accreditation.

A previous employer of mine, Arcus Global, introduced Volunteers Day, on which we were paid but spent time volunteering in the wider community. A colleague (Simon Cull) and I decided to volunteer with Code Club (https://codeclub. org/en) and we have not looked back. Despite us both moving on to other employers, we keep on doing our volunteering work as, at least for me, it improves my understanding of the broader field.

I also have some experience as a code mentor (Myers, 2018a) and have taught people who were engaged in a coding bootcamp. The students at the coding bootcamp had made a conscious decision to learn and used me to bolster that learning, and this further reinforced my understanding of the subject as well as theirs.

There are no formal universal accreditation schemes, but some come close to being so. It is worth researching any such schemes carefully to understand their prominence and recognition within the industry. Many providers of technology, such as Amazon and Salesforce, have accreditation schemes, but they are focused on those technologies and are perhaps not transferrable. There are more general training courses, and these might be better suited to you when you start your career. You could then focus on training for specific technologies if this will help your career progression.

Online course providers and books are also worth investigating, but again some care should be taken when it comes to accessing these resources: the field is continually evolving and what once was relevant might have been superseded. Newer versions of software might make older tutorials useless and leave you feeling frustrated and scouring further documentation.

Another source you can use to progress in your career is your colleagues. We explored the roles and responsibilities of other members of the development team in Chapter 1, and gaining a greater understanding of their work will help you and broaden your knowledge base. You can also help your colleagues to learn the skills you have mastered, though this should be done sensitively, so as not to appear patronising in any way. Some employers institute lunchtime meetings where learning can be disseminated among the team.

Alongside these impromptu, work-based conferences there are now many conferences and meetups aimed specifically at front-end developers. Wherever you live, you shouldn't find it too hard to meet up with other front-end developers, either to gain a more comprehensive understanding of the profession or to help you learn new techniques. You should also research and attend more formal conferences if possible. If you have the opportunity to present at one, then grasp the opportunity with both hands – it will increase your professional standing and force you to learn the nuts and bolts of the subject you're presenting.

MOVING ON FROM FRONT-END DEVELOPMENT

Due to the varied skill set required in front-end development, you will be exposed to a wide variety of technologies and processes in your role, allowing you to get a taste of possible avenues you might want to explore in greater depth.

If you lean more towards the overarching business where you are employed, then moving to a role such as product manager or owner will allow you to combine your existing expertise with a more business-oriented approach to the final product. If you lean more towards the user, then you might want to look at a role more focused on user experience or even design.

> There are greater and greater similarities between the tools used by designers and front-end developers, and this will help you significantly if you choose to go down this path.

Becoming a Scrum master might be another possible route and, should you want to explore more of the back-end and architecture, then becoming a software architect is a further possibility. With the increase in the use of JavaScript on the server, as well as NoSQL databases using data in a form analogous with JSON, front-end developers are also more than able to make the switch to back-end development or mix responsibilities by becoming full-stack developers.

Teaching is another possible avenue if it is something you enjoy. Considering the increasing popularity of web fundamentals courses, you might find that your experience is in demand. Helping to bring on future generations of front-end developers may well be something you find fulfilling.

As you can see, you have plenty of options should you wish to progress your career in an aligned area.

Carvill (2009) saw a lack of a clear career progression for front-end developers as worrying. He noted that there are only so many architect or senior engineer roles to go around, and only those developers who excel will be considered possible candidates. He suggested that one route would be to specialise in a specific aspect and work from there. Considering the pace at which the tools of our trade evolve, however, this might be more than a little problematic. You could become an expert in one framework or library, only to have it soon replaced by another, and the result could be finding yourself redundant.

One prediction Carvill made in 2009 – that performance specialists would be in higher demand in the five years after he wrote his article – only partly came to pass. Ubiquitous Wi-Fi, 4G and faster and faster devices mean that the need to simplify and reduce page loads is not so urgent. It is still essential but has become automated, either through software or via caching (on either the network or the device).

Many discussions of the career path of front-end developers note a progression from junior front-end developer to mid-level front-end developer through to senior front-end developer and then software designer or team lead and on to software architect or head of department, with technical fellow or chief technical officer (CTO) as a final step.

Software designer, software architect and technical fellow all have a distinct leaning towards a greater understanding of and facility with the technology associated with front-end development. In contrast, team lead, head of department and CTO have more of a leaning towards managerial responsibilities. Sometimes it is only through reading a job specification that you can adequately see whether you might be suited to a role, as different organisations will expect different things from the same job titles. This split does, however, illustrate that because we have two responsibilities (the business we work for and our audience), we are closely aligned with both spheres and our options are almost limitless within the software development field.

SUMMARY

As you can see, your options in terms of entering the profession, how you develop within your career, and where you might find yourself are varied. Enjoy the journey and learn to recognise when a path might be wrong for you. Save your attention for those things which will enrich your career and life. Learn from as many sources as you can and disseminate that knowledge widely while keeping the user as your focus.

6   CONCLUSION

It has never been so easy to learn front-end development. The number of resources available to you is almost overwhelming, and this is where you should be cautious, as it is easy to get distracted by older, stale resources which are not relevant to more modern development. Keeping the trinity of HTML, CSS and JavaScript in mind and reading around the subject should stand you in good stead.

Those coming to the front-end from other realms of development are sometimes appalled at the fast-and-loose nature of JavaScript. However, their desire to program in a stricter and statically typed language may be assuaged by using TypeScript or some other language that is transpilable to JavaScript. Indeed, the list of languages that compile to JavaScript (Ashkenas, 2018) suggests that no matter what style of programming you are comfortable with, you will probably find a method of converting it to JavaScript, if not now, then soon.

Being conversant in HTML, CSS and JavaScript, perhaps with a specialisation in either CSS or JavaScript, will mean that your job prospects are likely to remain excellent for the foreseeable future. Being conversant with both CSS and JavaScript might even make your HTML much more flexible; the current interest in native web components means that we are now more or less able to create or extend HTML elements in a way we once thought impossible. With a native web component, we can extend existing, or create new, HTML elements without having to include external libraries. Native web components are fascinating and represent a further union of HTML, CSS and JavaScript.

I thank you for your patience in reading this book. Front-end development is a relatively new field and one which is already becoming fragmented by its specialisations, but I hope I have offered something of a general introduction to the basics. Recently I have seen these basics discussed under the banner of 'web fundamentals', which, I guess, illustrates that this is merely a starting point and an indication that there is so very much more to learn.

Embrace that opportunity for learning and don't feel intimidated by it. I appreciate that it can sometimes feel overwhelming, but I, for one, find that the more I learn, the more comfortable I am learning. I would not go quite so far as Ed Hess (2014) when he says, 'Learn or Die'. However, if I ever felt like I had learnt everything there was to learn about a subject, I think it would be time to move on and learn something new. Experts I have known in other fields certainly echo this idea. In the realm of front-end development at least, there will always be something new to learn.

REFERENCES

Adobe, 2017. *How to Use Brackets – Live Preview*. [Online] Available at: https://github.com/adobe/brackets/wiki/How-to-Use-Brackets#live-preview.

Adobe, 2018. *Brackets – A Modern, Open Source Code Editor that Understands Web Design*. [Online] Available at: http://brackets.io.

Arkni, B. & Staab, M., 2018. *jQuery Validation Plugin*. [Online] Available at: https://jqueryvalidation.org.

Ashkenas, J., 2018. *List of Languages that Compile to JS*. [Online] Available at: https://github.com/jashkenas/coffeescript/wiki/List-of-languages-that-compile-to-JS.

Atlassian, 2018. *Sourcetree: Free Git GUI for Mac and Windows*. [Online] Available at: https://www.sourcetreeapp.com.

Austin, A., 2014. *An Overview of AngularJS for Managers*. [Online] Available at: https://andrewaustin.com/an-overview-of-angularjs-for-managers.

Avery, J., 2014. *Why You Don't Need Device Specific Breakpoints*. [Online] Available at: https://responsivedesign.is/articles/why-you-dont-need-device-specific-breakpoints.

Bailey, G., 2018. *Color Blindness: Types of Color Blindness*. [Online] Available at: https://www.allaboutvision.com/conditions/colordeficiency.htm.

BarelyFitz Designs, 2006. *Learn CSS Positioning in Ten Steps*. [Online] Available at: www.barelyfitz.com/screencast/html-training/css/positioning.

Barnett, C., 1963. *The Swordbearers: Studies in Supreme Command in the First World War*. London: Eyre and Spottiswoode.

BCS – The Chartered Institute for IT, 2015. *BCS Code of Conduct*. [Online] Available at: https://www.bcs.org/category/6030.

Biton, Y., 2018. *Point of Vue: Angular is Doomed, React is OK – We Deserve Better*. [Online] Available at: https://medium.com/@vyaron/point-of-vue-angular-is-doomed-react-is-ok-we-deserve-better-fb60652a8cb4.

Blankenship, D. C., 2010. *Applied Research and Evaluation Methods in Recreation*. Leeds: Human Kinetics.

Bostock, M., 2017. *Data-Driven Documents*. [Online] Available at: https://d3js.org.

Brocka, B., 2012. *What is the Best Practice for Data Table Cell Content Alignment – Answer ID 24073*. [Online] Available at: https://ux.stackexchange.com/questions/24066/what-is-the-best-practice-for-data-table-cell-content-alignment#24073.

Buckler, C., 2017. *Truthy and Falsy: When All is Not Equal in JavaScript*. [Online] Available at: https://www.sitepoint.com/javascript-truthy-falsy.

Buckler, C., 2018. *Understanding ES6 Modules*. [Online] Available at: https://www.sitepoint.com/understanding-es6-modules.

Carlton, 2016. *Impediments vs. Blockers – Why Make the Distinction?* [Online] Available at: https://lookforwardconsulting.com/2016/03/02/impediments-vs-blockers-why-make-the-distinction.

Carvill, P., 2009. *Why Front-End Developers are so Important to the Future of Businesses on the Web*. [Online] Available at: https://web.archive.org/web/20090926130100/https://www.paulcarvill.com/2009/09/why-front-end-developers-are-so-important-to-the-future-of-businesses-on-the-web.

Champeon, S., 2001. *JavaScript: How Did We Get Here?* [Online] Available at: https://web.archive.org/web/20160719020828/http:/archive.oreilly.com/pub/a/javascript/2001/04/06/js_history.html.

Cimpanu, C., 2018. *57% of Tech Workers are Suffering from Job Burnout*. [Online] Available at: https://www.bleepingcomputer.com/news/technology/57-percent-of-tech-workers-are-suffering-from-job-burnout/.

Citizens Advice, 2018. *If Your Employer Says You Owe Them Money – Citizens Advice*. [Online] Available at: https://www.citizensadvice.org.uk/work/leaving-a-job/resigning/if-your-employer-says-you-owe-them-money.

Codd, E. F. (1970). A Relational Model of Data for Large Shared Data Banks (PDF). *Communications of the ACM*, 13(6), pp. 377–387; 79(387), pp. 531–554.

Codesido, I., 2009. *What is Front-End Development?* [Online] Available at: https://www.theguardian.com/help/insideguardian/2009/sep/28/blogpost.

Computer History Museum, n.d. *The Babbage Engine*. [Online] Available at: www.computerhistory.org/babbage.

Coster, O., 2012. *Why is 80 Characters the 'Standard' Limit for Code Width? – Answer ID 148678*. [Online] Available at: https://softwareengineering.stackexchange.com/questions/148677/why-is-80-characters-the-standard-limit-for-code-width#148678.

Coyier, C., 2015. *Automatic CSS Testing*. [Online] Available at: https://css-tricks.com/automatic-css-testing.

Coyier, C., 2016. *Practical SVG*. n.p.: A Book Apart.

Coyier, C., 2018. *A Complete Guide to Flexbox*. [Online] Available at: https://css-tricks.com/snippets/css/a-guide-to-flexbox.

Creswell, J. W., 2008. *Educational Research: Planning, Conducting, and Evaluating Quantitative and Qualitative Research* (3rd ed.). Upper Saddle River: Prentice Hall.

Crockford, D., 2001. *JavaScript: The World's Most Misunderstood Programming Language*. [Online] Available at: http://crockford.com/javascript/javascript.html.

Cromwell, V., 2017. *Between the Wires: An Interview with Vue.js Creator Evan You*. [Online] Available at: https://medium.freecodecamp.org/between-the-wires-an-interview-with-vue-js-creator-evan-you-e383cbf57cc4.

CSS-Tricks, 2020. *A Complete Guide to Grid*. [Online] Available at: https://css-tricks.com/snippets/css/complete-guide-grid.

Cutrell, J., 2014. *7 CSS Units You Might Not Know About*. [Online] Available at: https://webdesign.tutsplus.com/articles/7-css-units-you-might-not-know-about--cms-22573.

Daniels, M., 2016. *The Case for Data Visualization*. [Online] Available at: https://www.viget.com/articles/the-case-for-data-visualization.

Davidson, D., 2014. *Why Do We Use Story Points for Estimating?* [Online] Available at: https://www.scrum.org/resources/blog/why-do-we-use-story-points-estimating.

Dayan, S., 2018. *Should You Chain or Extend CSS Classes?* [Online] Available at: https://frontstuff.io/should-you-chain-or-extend-css-classes.

Deveria, A., n.d.-a. *svg*. [Online] Available at: https://caniuse.com/#feat=svg.

Deveria, A., n.d.-b *vw*. [Online] Available at: https://caniuse.com/#search=vw.

Drasner, S., 2018. *Replacing jQuery with Vue.js: No Build Step Necessary*. [Online] Available at: https://www.smashingmagazine.com/2018/02/jquery-vue-javascript.

Dunn, K., 2018. *1. Visualizing Process Data – 1.7. Tables as a Form of Data Visualization*. [Online] Available at: https://learnche.org/pid/data-visualization/tables-as-a-form-of-data-visualization.

Editorial Team, 2016. *The Illustrated History of Web Forms*. [Online] Available at: https://1stwebdesigner.com/illustrated-history-of-web-forms.

Elliott, E., 2017. *Top JavaScript Libraries & Tech to Learn in 2018*. [Online] Available at: https://medium.com/javascript-scene/top-javascript-libraries-tech-to-learn-in-2018-c38028e028e6.

Estes, J., 2020. *Generative vs. Evaluation Research: What's the Difference and Why Do We Need Each?* [Online] Available at: https://www.usertesting.com/blog/generative-vs-evaluation-research.

Faulkner, S., 2016. *Consider Removing Table Sorting Model.* [Online] Available at: https://github.com/w3c/html/issues/56.

Few, S., 2007. *Save the Pies for Dessert.* [Online] Available at: www.perceptualedge.com/articles/08-21-07.pdf.

Ganguly, S., 2015. *Is Google Analytics Free of Charge?* [Online] Available at: https://webmasters.stackexchange.com/questions/81084/is-google-analytics-free-of-charge.

Garrett, J. J., 2005. *Ajax: A New Approach to Web Applications.* [Online] Available at: https://web.archive.org/web/20181231094556/https:/www.adaptivepath.com/ideas/ajax-new-approach-web-applications.

Gawron, K., 2016. *Infographic: JavaScript Tracking vs. Web Log Analytics.* [Online] Available at: https://piwik.pro/blog/javascript-tracking-web-log-analytics.

George, J., 2018. *Comparison with Other Frameworks.* [Online] Available at: https://vuejs.org/v2/guide/comparison.html#Angular-Formerly-known-as-Angular-2.

GIMP, 2018. *GIMP – GNU Image Manipulation Program.* [Online] Available at: https://www.gimp.org.

GitHub, 2018. *GitHub Desktop: Simple Collaboration from Your Desktop.* [Online] Available at: https://desktop.github.com.

Google, 2018. *Google HTML/CSS Style Guide – 3.2 HTML Formatting Rules – 3.2.2 HTML Line-Wrapping.* [Online] Available at: https://google.github.io/styleguide/htmlcssguide.html#HTML_Line-Wrapping.

GroetenUitDelft, 2011. *Scrum Master – Funny Movie about the Power of Scrum.* [Online] Available at: https://www.youtube.com/watch?v=P6v-I9VvTq4.

H, T. & V, V., n.d. *What Good Things Does Vue Take from React and Angular?* [Online] Available at: https://rubygarage.org/blog/things-vue-takes-from-react-and-angular.

Hamberg, S., 2018. *Why You Shouldn't Use Pie Charts – Tips for Better Data Visualization.* [Online] Available at: https://blog.funnel.io/why-we-dont-use-pie-charts-and-some-tips-on-better-data-visualizations.

Hamel, D., 2018a. *Boxer Text Editor – Built-In Syntax Highlighting Languages*. [Online] Available at: www.boxersoftware.com/pgfeat.htm.

Hamel, D., 2018b. *Texteditor.com – Boxer Text Editor for Windows*. [Online] Available at: www.boxersoftware.com/pgbwin.htm.

Harrin, E., 2017. *10 Ways to Overcome Imposter Syndrome*. [Online] Available at: https://www.girlsguidetopm.com/10-tips-to-overcome-imposter-syndrome.

Hartman, B., 2009. *Agile Pondering: Is it Agile to Have a 'Single Wringable Neck?'*. [Online] Available at: https://agileforall.com/agile-pondering-is-it-agile-to-have-a-single-wringable-neck.

Hertling, W., n.d. *Printing with CSS and Media Queries*. [Online] Available at: https://developers.hp.com/print-developers/doc/printing-css-and-media-queries.

Hess, E. D., 2014. *Learn or Die: Using Science to Build a Leading-Edge Learning Organization*. [Online] Available at: http://cup.columbia.edu/book/learn-or-die/9780231170246.

Hevery, M., n.d. *About Miško Hevery*. [Online] Available at: http://misko.hevery.com/about.

I'm Programmer, 2020. *Best Nosql Databases 2019 – Most Popular among Programmers*. [Online] Available at: https://www.improgrammer.net/most-popular-nosql-database.

International Cartographic Association, 2017. *Fig 10 11 Address Model*. [Online] Available at: https://wiki.icaci.org/index.php?title=File:Fig_10_11_Address_Model.png.

Jardine, A., 2018. *Add Advanced Interaction Controls to Your HTML Tables the Free & Easy Way*. [Online] Available at: https://datatables.net.

Javidx9, 2017. *What is Assembly Language?* [Online] Available at: https://www.youtube.com/watch?v=1FXhjErUz58.

Kosara, R., 2016. *Stacked Bars Are the Worst*. [Online] Available at: https://eagereyes.org/techniques/stacked-bars-are-the-worst.

Kyrnin, J., 2018. *CSS Vendor Prefixes*. [Online] Available at: https://www.lifewire.com/css-vendor-prefixes-3466867.

Lai, A., 2018. *Medoo – The Lightest PHP Database Framework to Accelerate Development*. [Online] Available at: https://medoo.in.

Landi, A., 2014. *Facing the Blank Canvas: Artists' Tips for Getting Started*. [Online] Available at: www.artnews.com/2014/06/23/artists-tips-for-facing-blank-canvas.

LeanKit, 2018. *Kanban vs. Scrum: What are the Differences?* [Online] Available at: https://leankit.com/learn/kanban/kanban-vs-scrum.

Lesswrongwiki, 2012. *The Map is Not the Territory*. [Online] Available at: https://wiki.lesswrong.com/wiki/The_map_is_not_the_territory.

Levkovsky, M., 2017. *Thinking in Redux (When All You've Known is MVC)*. [Online] Available at: https://hackernoon.com/thinking-in-redux-when-all-youve-known-is-mvc-c78a74d35133.

Lie, H. W., 1994. *Cascading HTML Style Sheets – A Proposal*. [Online] Available at: https://www.w3.org/People/howcome/p/cascade.html.

Magni, S., 2019. *New to Front-End Testing? Start from the Top of the Pyramid!* [Online] Available at: https://itnext.io/new-to-front-end-testing-start-from-the-top-of-the-pyramid-a0039615353c.

Mauer, G., 2017. HTML Forms' Time Has Come (Again). *CODE Magazine*, January/February.

Meiert, J. O., 2007. *User Agent Style Sheets: Basics and Samples*. [Online] Available at: https://meiert.com/en/blog/user-agent-style-sheets.

Microsoft, 2018. *Sketch2Code*. [Online] Available at: https://sketch2code.azurewebsites.net.

Modernizr, n.d. *What is Modernizr?* [Online] Available at: https://modernizr.com/docs/#what-is-modernizr.

Mortensen, D., 2018. *Conducting Ethical User Research*. [Online] Available at: https://www.interaction-design.org/literature/article/conducting-ethical-user-research.

Mozilla, 2019a. *<angle>*. [Online] Available at: https://developer.mozilla.org/en-US/docs/Web/CSS/angle.

Mozilla, 2019b. *<frequency>*. [Online] Available at: https://developer.mozilla.org/en-US/docs/Web/CSS/frequency.

Mozilla, 2019c. *<input type="tel">*. [Online] Available at: https://developer.mozilla.org/en-US/docs/Web/HTML/Element/input/tel.

Mozilla, 2019d. *<integer>*. [Online] Available at: https://developer.mozilla.org/en-US/docs/Web/CSS/integer.

Mozilla, 2019e. *<length>*. [Online] Available at: https://developer.mozilla.org/en-US/docs/Web/CSS/length.

Mozilla, 2019f. *<number>*. [Online] Available at: https://developer.mozilla.org/en-US/docs/Web/CSS/number.

Mozilla, 2019g. *<time>*. [Online] Available at: https://developer.mozilla.org/en-US/docs/Web/CSS/time.

Mozilla, 2019h. *REST*. [Online] Available at: https://developer.mozilla.org/en-US/docs/Glossary/REST.

Mozilla, 2020a. *calc()*. [Online] Available at: https://developer.mozilla.org/en-US/docs/Web/CSS/calc.

Mozilla, 2020b. *Classes*. [Online] Available at: https://developer.mozilla.org/en-US/docs/Web/JavaScript/Reference/Classes.

Mozilla, 2020c. *CSS: Cascading Style Sheets*. [Online] Available at: https://developer.mozilla.org/en-US/docs/Web/CSS.

Mozilla, 2020d. *CSS3*. [Online] Available at: https://developer.mozilla.org/en-US/docs/Web/CSS/CSS3.

Mozilla, 2020e. *for...in*. [Online] Available at: https://developer.mozilla.org/en-US/docs/Web/JavaScript/Reference/Statements/for...in.

Mozilla, 2020f. *<img>: The Image Embed Element*. [Online] Available at: https://developer.mozilla.org/en-US/docs/Web/HTML/Element/img.

Mozilla, 2020g. *Making Decisions in Your Code: Conditionals*. [Online] Available at: https://developer.mozilla.org/en-US/docs/Learn/JavaScript/Building_blocks/conditionals.

Mozilla, 2020h. *<percentage>*. [Online] Available at: https://developer.mozilla.org/en-US/docs/Web/CSS/percentage.

Mozilla, 2020i. *<template>: The Content Template Element*. [Online] Available at: https://developer.mozilla.org/en-US/docs/Web/HTML/Element/template.

Mozilla, 2020j. *What Are Browser Development Tools?* [Online] Available at: https://developer.mozilla.org/en-US/docs/Learn/Common_questions/What_are_browser_developer_tools.

Myers, D., 2010. *A Place for Amber*. [Online] Available at: http://drmsite.blogspot.com/2010/06/place-for-amber.html.

Myers, D., 2018a. *Dominic Myers*. [Online] Available at: https://www.codementor.io/annoyingmouse.

Myers, D., 2018b. *Getting IE11 to Play Nicely with Grid-Area*. [Online] Available at: http://drmsite.blogspot.com/2018/07/getting-ie11-to-play-nicely-with-grid.html.

Myers, D., 2018c. *User Test*. [Online] Available at: https://usertest-annoyingmouse.repl.co.

Network Working Group, 1996. *Request for Comments: 1942 – HTML Tables*. [Online] Available at: https://www.ietf.org/rfc/rfc1942.txt.

Noe, R., 2016. *What the UI Design of the Hawaii Missile Alert Actually Looks Like, and a Suggested Design Improvement ... and of Course, a Hilarious GIF Parody*. [Online] Available at: https://www.core77.com/posts/71766/What-the-UI-Design-of-the-Hawaii-Missile-Alert-Actually-Looks-Like-and-a-Suggested-Design-Improvement.

Oxford University Press, n.d. *Agile*. [Online] Available at: https://www.lexico.com/definition/agile.

Palas, P., 2017. *How I Built a CMS, and Why You Shouldn't.* [Online] Available at: https://hackernoon.com/how-i-built-a-cms-and-why-you-shouldnt-daff6042413a.

Paulb, 2012. *Using MS Word as a Code Editor.* [Online] Available at: https://superuser.com/questions/396139/using-ms-word-as-a-code-editor.

Petrosyan, M., 2018. *Angular 5 vs. React vs. Vue.* [Online] Available at: https://itnext.io/angular-5-vs-react-vs-vue-6b976a3f9172.

Pinar, 2017. *77-Year-Old Man 'Paints' Beautiful Japanese Landscapes on Excel Spreadsheets.* [Online] Available at: https://mymodernmet.com/tatsuo-horiuchi-excel-spreadsheet-paintings.

Plückthun, P., 2018. *What Sets Dank Mono Apart?* [Online] Available at: https://medium.com/@philpl/what-sets-dank-mono-apart-1bbdc1cc3cbd.

Poley, S., 2013. *The CSS Ex Unit.* [Online] Available at: https://sbpoley.home.xs4all.nl/webmatters/emex.html.

Polymer Project, 2018. *Polymer Project.* [Online] Available at: https://www.polymer-project.org.

Prowareness, 2018. *Home – Scrum.nl.* [Online] Available at: https://www.scrum.nl.

Radionov, V., 2017. *Understanding Stacked Bar Charts: The Worst or the Best?* [Online] Available at: https://www.smashingmagazine.com/2017/03/understanding-stacked-bar-charts.

Rand-Hendriksen, M., 2018. *Using Ethics in Web Design.* [Online] Available at: https://www.smashingmagazine.com/2018/03/using-ethics-in-web-design.

RIOT, 2018. *RIOT.* [Online] Available at: https://riot.js.org.

Robinson, D., 2017. *Developers Who Use Spaces Make More Money than Those Who Use Tabs.* [Online] Available at: https://stackoverflow.blog/2017/06/15/developers-use-spaces-make-money-use-tabs.

Sandeepsure, 2012. *Regular Expression for GB Based and Only Numeric Phone Number.* [Online] Available at: https://stackoverflow.com/questions/11518035/regular-expression-for-gb-based-and-only-numeric-phone-number.

Sanderson, S., n.d. *Knockout.* [Online] Available at: https://knockoutjs.com.

Schier, G., 2013. *JavaScript Method Chaining.* [Online] Available at: https://schier.co/blog/method-chaining-in-javascript.

Schouten, A., 2015. *HTML Boolean Attributes List.* [Online] Available at: https://gist.github.com/ArjanSchouten/0b8574a6ad7f5065a5e7.

Scrum Alliance, 2018. *Professional Scrum & Agile Training & Certifications – Scrum Alliance.* [Online] Available at: https://www.scrumalliance.org.

Sempf, B., 2014. *Bill Sempf.* [Online] Available at: https://twitter.com/sempf/status/514473420277694465?lang=en.

Shariat, J., 2014. *How Bad UX Killed Jenny.* [Online] Available at: https://medium.com/tragic-design/how-bad-ux-killed-jenny-ef915419879e.

Shea, D., 2005. *CSS Zen Garden – The Beauty of CSS Design.* [Online] Available at: www.csszengarden.com.

Sherwin, K., 2018. *Placeholders in Form Fields are Harmful.* [Online] Available at: https://www.nngroup.com/articles/form-design-placeholders.

Sims, G., 2016. *Assembly Language and Machine Code.* [Online] Available at: https://www.youtube.com/watch?v=wA2oMRmbrfo.

Skorkin, A., 2010. *The Difference between a Developer, a Programmer and a Computer Scientist.* [Online] Available at: https://skorks.com/2010/03/the-difference-between-a-developer-a-programmer-and-a-computer-scientist.

Stack Overflow, 2019. *How to Set HTML5 Required Attribute in JavaScript?* [Online] Available at: https://stackoverflow.com/questions/18770369/how-to-set-html5-required-attribute-in-javascript.

Stepanov, K., 2017. *How to Retain Ethics in Web Development and Not Sell Out*. [Online] Available at: https://medium.com/shakuro/how-to-retain-ethics-in-web-development-and-not-sell-out-aae1abc6527c.

Sturgeon, P., 2017. *GraphQL vs REST: Overview*. [Online] Available at: https://philsturgeon.uk/api/2017/01/24/graphql-vs-rest-overview.

Sublime HQ Pty Ltd, 2018. *Sublime Text – A Sophisticated Text Editor for Code, Markup and Prose*. [Online] Available at: https://www.sublimetext.com.

Sutherland, J. & Schwaber, K., 2018. *Home: Scrum Guides*. [Online] Available at: https://www.scrumguides.org.

Tableau Software, 2018. *Tableau: Business Intelligence and Analytics Software*. [Online] Available at: https://www.tableau.com.

Thayer, K., 2017. *What I Learned from Researching Coding Bootcamps*. [Online] Available at: https://medium.com/bits-and-behavior/what-i-learned-from-researching-coding-bootcamps-f594c15bd9e0.

Thayer, K., 2018. *Coding Bootcamps vs. Computer Science Degrees: What Employers Want and Other Perspectives*. [Online] Available at: https://medium.com/bits-and-behavior/coding-bootcamps-vs-computer-science-degrees-what-employers-want-and-other-perspectives-4058a67e4f15.

The Guardian, 2011. *Megas – Winners 2011*. [Online] Available at: https://www.theguardian.com/megas/winners-2011.

Thinkwik, 2017. *Why You should Use AngularJS for Your Front-End Development*. [Online] Available at: https://medium.com/@thinkwik/why-you-should-use-angularjs-for-your-front-end-development-cdbeb876cc40.

ThoughtWorks, 2018. *Technology Radar*. [Online] Available at: https://www.thoughtworks.com/radar.

Tilde Inc., 2018. *Ember – A Framework for Ambitious Web Developers*. [Online] Available at: https://www.emberjs.com.

Tyson, J. & Carmack, C., 2000. *How Computer Monitors Work.* [Online] Available at: https://computer.howstuffworks.com/monitor2.htm.

Underscore, 2018. *Underscore.js.* [Online] Available at: https://underscorejs.org.

Value Coders, 2018. *Vue.js is Good, but is it Better than Angular or React?* [Online] Available at: https://www.valuecoders.com/blog/technology-and-apps/vue-js-comparison-angular-react.

Viola, 2012. *Making the Background of an Image Transparent in Gimp.* [Online] Available at: https://graphicdesign.stackexchange.com/questions/5446/making-the-background-of-an-image-transparent-in-gimp.

Vo, T., 2015. *A Conversation with Norm Cox, Creator of the Hamburger Menu.* [Online] Available at: https://medium.com/readme-mic/a-conversation-with-norm-cox-creator-of-the-hamburger-menu-c913daea5f9e.

W3C, 1991. *HTML Tags.* [Online] Available at: https://www.w3.org/History/19921103-hypertext/hypertext/WWW/MarkUp/Tags.html.

W3C, 1999. *11 Tables – 11.1 Introduction to Tables.* [Online] Available at: https://www.w3.org/TR/1999/REC-html401-19991224/struct/tables.html#h-11.1.

W3C, 2011. *HTML5 – The Placeholder Attribute.* [Online] Available at: https://www.w3.org/TR/2011/WD-html5-20110525/common-input-element-attributes.html#the-placeholder-attribute.

W3C, 2017a. *CSS Grid Layout Module Level 1 – 7.2.3. Flexible Lengths: The Fr Unit.* [Online] Available at: https://www.w3.org/TR/css3-grid-layout/#fr-unit.

W3C, 2017b. *4.9. Tabular Data – 4.9.1. The Table Element.* [Online] Available at: https://www.w3.org/TR/html52/tabular-data.html#the-table-element.

W3C, 2018. *CSS Values and Units Module Level 3 – 5.1.2. Viewport-Percentage Lengths: The Vw, Vh, Vmin, Vmax Units.*

[Online] Available at: https://www.w3.org/TR/css-values-3/#viewport-relative-lengths.

W3C, 2019. *Forms Concepts*. [Online] Available at: https://www.w3.org/WAI/tutorials/forms.

W3Schools, 2020a. *CSS Display Property*. [Online] Available at: https://www.w3schools.com/cssref/pr_class_display.asp.

W3Schools, 2020b. *CSS Introduction*. [Online] Available at: https://www.w3schools.com/css/css_intro.asp.

W3Schools, 2020c. *SQL Injection*. [Online] Available at: https://www.w3schools.com/sql/sql_injection.asp.

W3Schools, 2020d. *SVG in HTML*. [Online] Available at: https://www.w3schools.com/graphics/svg_inhtml.asp.

W3Schools, 2020e. *XML Parser*. [Online] Available at: https://www.w3schools.com/xml/xml_parser.asp.

W3Techs, n.d. *Usage Statistics and Market Share of jQuery for Websites*. [Online] Available at: https://w3techs.com/technologies/details/js-jquery/all/all.

WAA Standards Committee, 2008. *Web Analytics Definitions*. Washington, DC: Web Analytics Association.

Waters, K., 2007. *Agile Principle 7: Done Means DONE!* [Online] Available at: https://www.101ways.com/2007/04/08/agile-principle-7-done-means-done.

Weinstock-Herman, E., 2011. *The History of HTML Table Layouts*. [Online] Available at: http://blogs.lessthandot.com/index.php/webdev/uidevelopment/xhtmlcss/history-of-html-table-layouts.

WhatsTheHost Team, 2019. *Coding Bootcamp vs. Computer Science Degree [Infographic]*. [Online] Available at: https://www.whatsthehost.com/coding-bootcamp-vs-cs-degree.

Wikipedia, 2018. *Front-End Web Development*. [Online] Available at: https://en.wikipedia.org/w/index.php?title=Front-end_web_development.

Wikipedia, 2020b. *High-Level Programming Language.* [Online] Available at: https://en.wikipedia.org/w/index.php?title=High-level_programming_language&oldid=872185462.

Wikipedia, 2020c. *Interpreted Language.* [Online] Available at: https://en.wikipedia.org/w/index.php?title=Interpreted_language.

Wikipedia, 2020d. *JavaScript.* [Online] Available at: https://en.wikipedia.org/w/index.php?title=JavaScript.

Wikipedia, 2020e. *Microsoft Visual Studio – Editions – Community.* [Online] Available at: https://en.wikipedia.org/w/index.php?title=Microsoft_Visual_Studio.

Wikipedia, 2020f. *Separation of Concerns.* [Online] Available at: https://en.wikipedia.org/w/index.php?title=Separation_of_concerns.

Wikipedia, 2020g. *The Lean Startup.* [Online] Available at: https://en.wikipedia.org/w/index.php?title=The_Lean_Startup.

Wikipedia, 2020a. *Comparison of Web Template Engines.* [Online] Available at: https://en.wikipedia.org/w/index.php?title=Comparison_of_web_template_engines.

Wilson, R. A., 1977. *Cosmic Trigger I: The Final Secret of the Illuminati.* Grand Junction, CO: Hilaritas Press.

Wroblewski, L., 2005. *Web Application Form Design.* [Online] Available at: https://www.lukew.com/ff/entry.asp?1502.

Wyse, J., 2014. *Why JSON is Better than XML.* [Online] Available at: https://blog.cloud-elements.com/json-better-xml.

Yau, N., 2018. *FlowingData.* [Online] Available at: https://flowingdata.com.

Yellvula, N., 2017. *Why Full Stack Development is Too Good for You in 2017.* [Online] Available at: https://medium.com/dev-bits/why-full-stack-development-is-too-good-for-you-in-2017-3fd6fe207b34.

Yerburgh, E., 2017. *The Front-End Test Pyramid: How to Rethink Your Testing*. [Online] Available at: https://www.freecodecamp. org/news/the-front-end-test-pyramid-rethink-your-testing-3b343c2bca51.

Zakas, N. C., 2005. *Professional JavaScript for Web Developers*. Indianapolis: Wrox.

FURTHER READING

AlternativeTo, n.d. *DataTables Alternatives and Similar Software*. [Online] Available at: https://alternativeto.net/software/datatables.

Arnott, S. & Haskin, M., 2004. *Man Walks into a Bar: The Ultimate Collection of Jokes and One-Liners*. London: Ebury.

Arrk Group, 2018. *Fail Fast, Fail Often: Explained*. [Online] Available at: https://www.arrkgroup.com/thought-leadership/fail-fast-fail-often-explained.

Ashanin, N., 2017. *The Path to Becoming a Software Architect*. [Online] Available at: https://medium.com/@nvashanin/the-path-to-becoming-a-software-architect-de53f1cb310a.

Avery, J., 2017. *Media Queries for Common Device Breakpoints*. [Online] Available at: https://responsivedesign.is/develop/browser-feature-support/media-queries-for-common-device-breakpoints.

Awio Web Services LLC, n.d. *Web Browser Usage Trends*. [Online] Available at: https://www.w3counter.com/trends.

Balsamiq Studios LLC, 2018. *Balsamiq: Rapid, Effective and Fun Wireframing Software*. [Online] Available at: https://balsamiq.com.

Berners-Lee, T., n.d. *The WorldWideWeb Browser*. [Online] Available at: https://www.w3.org/People/Berners-Lee/WorldWideWeb.html.

Bersvendsen, A., 2005. *Who Created CSS? CSS Early History*. [Online] Available at: https://virtuelvis.com/2005/01/who-created-css-css-early-history.

Bootstrap, 2018. *Bootstrap*. [Online] Available at: https://getbootstrap.com.

Bruce, R. & Jacobs, N., 2013. *Ten Search Engines for Researchers that Go beyond Google*. [Online] Available at: https://www.jisc.ac.uk/blog/ten-search-engines-for-researchers-that-go-beyond-google-11-jul-2013.

Burger, N., 2018. *The End of Life of Internet Explorer 11*. [Online] Available at: https://nealbuerger.com/2018/01/the-end-of-life-of-internet-explorer-11.

Chakrabortty, A., 2018. Mis-sold, Expensive and Overhyped: Why Our Universities are a Con. *The Guardian*, 20 September.

Chapman, S., 2017. *Learn about the Early History of the Java Programming Language*. [Online] Available at: https://www.thoughtco.com/a-brief-history-of-javascript-2037675.

Chedygov, S., 2009. *Differences between Emacs and Vim*. [Online] Available at: https://stackoverflow.com/questions/1430164/differences-between-emacs-and-vim.

Cleveland, W. S. & McGill, R., 1983. Graphical Perception: Theory, Experimentation, and Application to the Development of Graphical Methods. *Journal of the American Statistical Association*, 79(387), pp. 531–554.

Czaplicki, E., 2018. *Elm – A Delightful Language for Reliable Webapps*. [Online] Available at: https://elm-lang.org.

Data & Object Factory, 2018. *Chain of Responsibility*. [Online] Available at: https://www.dofactory.com/javascript/chain-of-responsibility-design-pattern.

Devin, 2017. *Are Horizontal Forms Ever Good UX? – Answer ID 108732*. [Online] Available at: https://ux.stackexchange.com/questions/108730/are-horizontal-forms-ever-good-ux/108732#108732.

DiNucci, D., 1999. Fragmented Future. *Print Magazine*, 4(32), pp. 221–222.

Dybå, T., 2008. *Empirical Studies of Agile Software Development: A Systematic Review*. [Online] Available at: https://www.sciencedirect.com/science/article/abs/pii/S0950584908000256.

Ecma International, 2018. *TC39 – ECMAScript®*. [Online] Available at: https://www.ecma-international.org/memento/tc39-m.htm.

Education Technology, 2018. *Music Education vs. Education Technology*. [Online] Available at: https://edtechnology.co.uk/Blog/music-education-vs-education-technology.

Elliott, E., 2016. *You Might Not Need TypeScript (or Static Types)*. [Online] Available at: https://medium.com/javascript-scene/you-might-not-need-typescript-or-static-types-aa7cb670a77b.

Ely Makers, 2018. *Ely Makers*. [Online] Available at: www.elymakers.co.uk.

Fenner, S., n.d. *What is an Organogram? Definition, Structure & Example*. [Online] Available at: https://study.com/academy/lesson/what-is-an-organogram-definition-structure-example.html.

Ferreira, J., 2018. *United Kingdom Unemployment Rate*. [Online] Available at: https://tradingeconomics.com/united-kingdom/unemployment-rate.

Fileformat.info, 2018. *Unicode Character 'HORIZONTAL TAB KEY' (U+2B7E)*. [Online] Available at: https://www.fileformat.info/info/unicode/char/2b7e/index.htm.

Filipova, O., 2017. *Vue.js 2 and Bootstrap 4 Web Development*. Birmingham: Packt.

Gallagher, P., 2012. Revealed: How the Cost of a Degree is Now £100,000. *The Independent*, 9 December.

Gao, Z., Bird, C. & Barr, E. T., 2017. *To Type or Not to Type: Quantifying Detectable Bugs in JavaScript*. [Online] Available at: http://ttendency.cs.ucl.ac.uk/projects/type_study/documents/type_study.pdf.

Goldfarb, C., 1993. *SGML Users' Group History*. [Online] Available at: http://xml.coverpages.org/sgmlhist0.html.

Gonzalo, A. G., 2011. *Hildegard E. Peplau: Interpersonal Relations Theory*. [Online] Available at: https://nurseslabs.com/hildegard-peplaus-interpersonal-relations-theory.

Graduate Recruitment Bureau, n.d. *The 7 Benefits of Hiring Graduates*. [Online] Available at: https://www.grb.uk.com/recruiter-research/7-benefits-of-hiring-graduates.

Granger, C., 2014. *Toward a Better Programming*. [Online] Available at: www.chris-granger.com/2014/03/27/toward-a-better-programming.

Greenspun, P., n.d. *Netscape LiveWire*. [Online] Available at: http://philip.greenspun.com/wtr/livewire.html.

Grobe, M., 1997. *An Early History of Lynx: Multidimensional Collaboration*. [Online] Available at: http://people.cc.ku.edu/~grobe/early-lynx.html.

Hanselman, S., 2012. *The Floppy Disk Means Save, and 14 Other Old People Icons that Don't Make Sense Anymore*. [Online] Available at: https://www.hanselman.com/blog/TheFloppyDiskMeansSaveAnd14OtherOld PeopleIconsThatDontMakeSenseAnymore.aspx.

Harari, Y. N., 2018. *21 Lessons for the 21st Century*. London: Jonathan Cape.

Hayden, B. Y., 2014. *Do We Need Work to be Happy?* [Online] Available at: https://www.psychologytoday.com/gb/blog/the-decision-tree/201404/do-we-need-work-be-happy.

hcspider, 2017. *Front End Developer Career Path*. [Online] Available at: https://www.reddit.com/r/Frontend/comments/5yd38h/front_end_developer_career_path.

Hickson, I., n.d. *Acid Tests*. [Online] Available at: www.acidtests.org.

Higginbottom, K., 2018. *Two-Thirds of Women in U.K. Suffer from Imposter Syndrome at Work*. [Online] Available at: https://www.forbes.com/sites/karenhigginbottom/2018/07/29/two-thirds-of-women-in-uk-suffer-from-imposter-syndrome-at-work/#5dab8bcb6ccf.

Hogenboom, M., 2018. *What Does Your Accent Say About You?* [Online] Available at: www.bbc.com/future/story/20180307-what-does-your-accent-say-about-you.

Holland, B., 2018. *Hand Roll Charts with D3 Like You Actually Know What You're Doing*. [Online] Available at: https://css-tricks.com/hand-roll-charts-with-d3-like-you-actually-know-what-youre-doing.

Hughes, M., 2000. *Mastering Systems Analysis Design*. London: Macmillan Education.

International Cartographic Association, 2017. *ISO 19160-1:2015 Addressing – Part 1: Conceptual Model*. [Online] Available at: https://wiki.icaci.org/index.php?title=ISO_19160-1:2015_Addressing_-_Part_1:_Conceptual_model.

IT Jobs Watch Ltd, 2018. *Front End Developer (Client-Side Developer) UK*. [Online] Available at: https://www.itjobswatch.co.uk/contracts/uk/front-end%20developer.do.

Jardine, A., 2018. *Installation – HTML*. [Online] Available at: https://datatables.net/manual/installation#HTML.

Jobson, C., 2017. *Meet Tatsuo Horiuchi, the 77-Year-Old Artist Who 'Paints' Japanese Landscapes with Excel*. [Online] Available at: https://www.thisiscolossal.com/2017/12/tatsuo-horiuchi-excel-artist.

jQuery Foundation, 2018. *jQuery: The Write Less, Do More, JavaScript Library*. [Online] Available at: http://jquery.com.

Keyes, L. & McAllister, K., 2016. *Nurses as Change Agents*. [Online] Available at: https://www.mastersinnursing.com/nurses-as-change-agents.

Kirby, P., 2016. *Degrees of Debt*. [Online] Available at: https://www.suttontrust.com/research-paper/degrees-of-debt-student-finance-comparison.

Kyrnin, J., 2018. *Why You should Avoid Tables for Web Page Layouts*. [Online] Available at: https://www.lifewire.com/dont-use-tables-for-layout-3468941.

Lambert, S., 2013. *An Introduction to Spritesheet Animation*. [Online] Available at: https://gamedevelopment.tutsplus.com/tutorials/an-introduction-to-spritesheet-animation-gamedev-13099.

Lee, N., 2017. *Configuring Sublime Text 3 for Modern ES6 JS Projects.* [Online] Available at: https://medium.com/@nicklee1/configuring-sublime-text-3-for-modern-es6-js-projects-6f3fd69e95de.

Liao, S., 2018. *Hawaii's Missile Alert Interface Had a One-Word Difference between Sending a Test Alert and a Real One.* [Online] Available at: https://www.theverge.com/2018/1/16/16896368/hawaii-false-missile-alert-system-confusing-interface-poor-design.

Liddle, G., 2013. *Why Agile is so Popular: Are You Ready?* [Online] Available at: www.us.cgi.com/blog/2013/12/16/why-agile-is-so-popular-are-you-ready-to-be-agile.

lipsum.com, n.d. *Lorem Ipsum.* [Online] Available at: https://www.lipsum.com.

Lull, D., 2017. *Discussions in User Experience – Healthcare for User Frustration.* Berkeley, CA: Springer.

marcgise, 2017. *Datatables with Vue.js?* [Online] Available at: https://datatables.net/forums/discussion/42571/datatables-with-vue-js.

Merlin, M., n.d. *Mosaic for X Version 2.0 Fill-Out Form Support.* [Online] Available at: http://marc.merlins.org/htmlearn/forms/forms.html.

Microsoft, 2018. *Playground.* [Online] Available at: www.typescriptlang.org/play/index.html.

Microsoft, 2018. *Visual Studio Code – Code Editing. Redefined.* [Online] Available at: https://code.visualstudio.com.

Mönnich, A., 2013. *What is VanillaJS?* [Online] Available at: https://stackoverflow.com/questions/20435653/what-is-vanillajs#20435744.

Moore, B., n.d. *JsRender.* [Online] Available at: https://www.jsviews.com/#jsrender.

Mozilla, 2018. *calc() – Accessibility Concerns.* [Online] Available at: https://developer.mozilla.org/en-US/docs/Web/CSS/calc#Accessibility_concerns.

Mozilla, 2018. *Data URLs*. [Online] Available at: https://developer.mozilla.org/en-US/docs/Web/HTTP/Basics_of_HTTP/Data_URIs.

Mozilla, 2018. *HTTP Request Methods*. [Online] Available at: https://developer.mozilla.org/en-US/docs/Web/HTTP/Methods.

Mozilla, 2018. *Web APIs*. [Online] Available at: https://developer.mozilla.org/en-US/docs/Web/API.

Myers, D., 2008. *Example Macros – Convert Small GIFs to BASE64 for Use in Mozilla URLs*. [Online] Available at: www.boxersoftware.com/pgmacros.shtml#macro31.

Myers, D., 2015. *How to Display a Bar Chart in DataTable*. [Online] Available at: https://stackoverflow.com/questions/30997562/how-to-display-a-bar-chart-in-datatable/31003426#31003426.

Myers, D., 2017. *Should I Get Involved in a Code Club?* [Online] Available at: https://www.bcs.org/content/conBlogPost/2699.

Myers, D., 2018. *SGMLguid – Original*. [Online] Available at: https://jsfiddle.net/annoyingmouse/e97htuow.

Myers, D., 2018. *SGMLguid – Updated*. [Online] Available at: https://jsfiddle.net/annoyingmouse/vr8fdzw9.

Myers, D. & Cull, S., 2018. *Frogger in p5 and ES6*. [Online] Available at: https://github.com/annoyingmouse/WireFrameJS/tree/master/000-MISCELLANEOUS/p5FROGGER.

Myers, D. & Cull, S., 2018. *Snake Using p5*. [Online] Available at: https://github.com/annoyingmouse/WireFrameJS/tree/master/000-MISCELLANEOUS/p5SNAKE.

Nadir, S. S., 2017. *Javascript Function Chaining: How jQuery Ruled the Web*. [Online] Available at: https://medium.com/@saginadir/native-function-chaining-in-javascript-what-we-can-learn-from-jquery-3b42d5d4a0d.

Network Working Group, 1995. *Hypertext Markup Language – 2.0*. [Online] Available at: https://www.rfc-editor.org/rfc/rfc1866.txt.

Newton, A., 2009. *jQuery vs MooTools*. [Online] Available at: www.jqueryvsmootools.com/#conclusion.

Nichols, K., n.d. *JavaScript is Not Java*. [Online] Available at: http://javascriptisnotjava.com.

Palmer, S. B., n.d. *The Early History of HTML*. [Online] Available at: http://infomesh.net/html/history/early.

Pearson, B., 2010. *History of HTML Tables – Introduction*. [Online] Available at: www.barrypearson.co.uk/articles/layout_tables/history.htm.

Pisarev, K., 2014. *How to Chain in Javascript without Jquery?* [Online] Available at: https://stackoverflow.com/questions/27701156/how-to-chain-in-javascript-without-jquery#27701197.

Raggett, D., Lam, J., Alexander, I. & Kmiec, M., 1998. *2 – A History of HTML*. [Online] Available at: https://www.w3.org/People/Raggett/book4/ch02.html.

Rana, S., 2017. *Will Robots Take Away All Our Jobs in the Next 20 Years?* [Online] Available at: https://www.futureofeverything.io/will-robots-take-away-jobs-next-20-years.

Raspberry Pi Foundation, 2018. *How Computers Work: Demystifying Computation*. [Online] Available at: https://www.futurelearn.com/courses/how-computers-work.

Romanik, B., 2013. *Why the Best Programmers Are Lazy and Act Dumb*. [Online] Available at: https://www.techwell.com/techwell-insights/2013/12/why-best-programmers-are-lazy-and-act-dumb.

Sanders, J., 2018. *Why It's Finally Time to Give Up on the Name JavaScript*. [Online] Available at: https://www.techrepublic.com/article/why-its-finally-time-to-give-up-on-the-name-javascript.

Sauer, J., 2018. *Data Driven*. [Online] Available at: https://www.datadrivenu.com.

Scherer, R., Siddiq, F. & Viveros, B. S., 2018. The Cognitive Benefits of Learning Computer Programming: A Meta-analysis of Transfer Effects. *Journal of Educational Psychology*, 111(5), pp. 764–792.

Sharp, R., 2010. *What is a Polyfill?* [Online] Available at: https://remysharp.com/2010/10/08/what-is-a-polyfill.

Smith, L., 2017. *Why Women Experience 'Impostor Syndrome' – and How to Beat it.* [Online] Available at: https://www.cosmopolitan.com/uk/reports/a12029501/impostor-syndrome-women-what-is-it-how-to-beat-it.

Stack Overflow, n.d. *Annoyingmouse.* [Online] Available at: https://stackoverflow.com/users/592058/annoyingmouse.

Tabalin, A., 2016. *jsGrid.* [Online] Available at: http://js-grid.com.

The Health Foundation, 1992. *The Health of the Nation – A Strategy for Health in England White Paper was Published.* [Online] Available at: https://navigator.health.org.uk/content/health-nation-%E2%80%93-strategy-health-england-white-paper-was-published.

Tobak, S., 2017. *Why 'Fail Fast, Fail Often' is All Hype.* [Online] Available at: https://www.entrepreneur.com/article/288147.

Trow, J., 2015. *Responsive CSS Only Animated Bar Graph.* [Online] Available at: https://codepen.io/jedtrow/pen/YPrqKY.

VanToll, T. J., 2012. *Constraint Validation: Native Client Side Validation for Web Forms.* [Online] Available at: https://www.html5rocks.com/en/tutorials/forms/constraintvalidation.

W3C, 2012. *3. Documents.* [Online] Available at: http://w3c.github.io/html-reference/documents.html.

W3C, 2012. *Web Ontology Language (OWL).* [Online] Available at: https://www.w3.org/OWL.

W3Schools, 2020. *CSS Media Queries – Examples.* [Online] Available at: https://www.w3schools.com/css/css3_mediaqueries_ex.asp.

W3Schools, 2020. *XSLT Introduction.* [Online] Available at: https://www.w3schools.com/xml/xsl_intro.asp.

Wales, M., 2014. *3 Web Dev Careers Decoded: Front-End vs Back-End vs Full Stack.* [Online] Available at: https://blog.udacity.com/2014/12/front-end-vs-back-end-vs-full-stack-web-developers.html.

Wastl, E., n.d. *Vanilla JS*. [Online] Available at: http://vanilla-js.com.

Webb, R., 2013. *The Economics of* Star Trek. [Online] Available at: https://medium.com/@RickWebb/the-economics-of-star-trek-29bab88d50.

Webopedia Staff, n.d. *Java Applet.* [Online] Available at: https://www.webopedia.com/TERM/J/Java_applet.html.

Wikipedia, 2020. *Bert Bos.* [Online] Available at: https://en.wikipedia.org/w/index.php?title=Bert_Bos.

Wikipedia, 2020. *Canvas Element – Canvas versus Scalable Vector Graphics (SVG).* [Online] Available at: https://en.wikipedia.org/w/index.php?title=Canvas_element#Canvas_versus_Scalable_Vector_Graphics_(SVG).

Wikipedia, 2020. *Douglas Crockford.* [Online] Available at: https://en.wikipedia.org/w/index.php?title=Douglas_Crockford.

Wikipedia, 2020. *Edgar F. Codd.* [Online] Available at: https://en.wikipedia.org/w/index.php?title=Edgar_F._Codd.

Wikipedia, 2020. *GIF – Pronunciation of GIF.* [Online] Available at: https://en.wikipedia.org/w/index.php?title=GIF#Pronunciation_of_GIF.

Wikipedia, 2020. *Håkon Wium Lie.* [Online] Available at: https://en.wikipedia.org/w/index.php?title=H%C3%A5kon_Wium_Lie.

Wikipedia, 2020. *HSL and HSV.* [Online] Available at: https://en.wikipedia.org/w/index.php?title=HSL_and_HSV.

Wikipedia, 2020. *Jesse James Garrett.* [Online] Available at: https://en.wikipedia.org/w/index.php?title=Jesse_James_Garrett.

Wikipedia, 2020. *John W. Creswell.* [Online] Available at: https://en.wikipedia.org/w/index.php?title=John_W._Creswell.

Wikipedia, 2020. *NoSQL – History.* [Online] Available at: https://en.wikipedia.org/w/index.php?title=NoSQL#History.

Wikipedia, 2020. *Right to Internet Access*. [Online] Available at: https://en.wikipedia.org/w/index.php?title=Right_to_Internet_ access.

Wikipedia, 2020. *Web 2.0 – Web 2.0 – Characteristics*. [Online] Available at: https://en.wikipedia.org/w/index.php?title=Web_ 2.0#Characteristics_2.

Wikipedia, 2020. *Web Analytics – Basic Steps of Web Analytics Process*. [Online] Available at: https://en.wikipedia.org/w/ index.php?title=Web_analytics#/media/File:Basic_Steps_of_ Web_Analytics_Process.png.

Wikipedia, 2020. *Web Design – Evolution of Web Design*. [Online] Available at: https://en.wikipedia.org/w/index.php?title=Web_ design#Evolution_of_web_design.

Wikipedia, 2020. *XQuery*. [Online] Available at: https:// en.wikipedia.org/w/index.php?title=XQuery.

Wikipedia, 2020. *Yuval Noah Harari*. [Online] Available at: https:// en.wikipedia.org/w/index.php?title=Yuval_Noah_Harari.

GLOSSARY

Acceptance testing: Testing that aims to ensure that the software meets the requirements initially specified.

Agile: A team-based software development methodology designed to embrace change and speed.

Angular: A JavaScript framework, most usually written in TypeScript.

Application programming interface (API): An API is a messaging service between computer systems, allowing a computer to make requests and receive responses.

Aspect ratio: The ratio of the width of an image to its height, separated by a colon. A square image would have an aspect ratio of 1:1. The numbers are always as low as possible, in the same way as fractions are reduced. For example, if an image was 1440px wide and 960px tall, it would have an aspect ratio of 3:2.

Assembly language: Assembly languages are processor specific and closely resemble instructions to the CPU. They are not very user friendly, so higher-level languages were developed. See Javidx9 (2017) for lots more information.

Asynchronous JavaScript and XML (AJAX): AJAX allows a JavaScript program to communicate with a server without having to submit a form. One way to think of it is that the browser takes multiple sips of data from the server rather than huge gulps.

Attribute: While some HTML elements don't require attributes, some, such as `img` and `source`, would be useless without them. They either act as a modifier to the attribute or provide functionality.

Back-end: For front-end developers, the back-end is most usually the server and any programs or databases running there.

Backlog: All the work yet to be completed and not yet scheduled. In Agile, all tasks start in the backlog before being completed.

Base64: An encoding algorithm. It uses a base-64 numbering system rather than the decimal (base-10) system you will be more familiar with. It is most often used to convert binary data, such as images, into text but it can also be used to convert other types of data.

Boolean: A Boolean value is either `true` or `false` (0 or 1). There are other value types, such as numbers and strings, and these can be tested using Boolean tests. For instance, `1 === 1` would result in `true` whereas `1 === 2` would result in `false`. In JavaScript, there are the concepts of 'truthy' and 'falsy', as it is a dynamically typed language. This can trip up developers, but Craig Buckler (2017) has an excellent resource with further information.

Bundler: A bundler bundles multiple JavaScript files into one. It ensures that any programming dependencies are loaded and available before they are required by other parts of the program.

Business logic: Business logic deals with how data can be created, read, updated and deleted (often shortened to CRUD), usually in a database on the back-end.

Call: The process of making an API request.

Cascading Style Sheets (CSS): The language used to style HTML markup.

Chaining: Chaining in CSS is the way in which multiple classes are added to an element to change its style. Chaining in JavaScript is used in jQuery. You can incorporate it into your own code and it is accomplished by returning the object after each method call. Gregory Schier (2013) goes into far greater depth on his blog.

Child: The nested nature of HTML means that all elements are the children of the main `html` element. Most other elements can also have children, but some cannot. Reading the document type definition will tell you which can, and also what their accepted children are.

Class: In CSS, a `class` is an attribute and identifier of one or more elements, as opposed to an `id` attribute: there should only ever be one element with a given `id`. In JavaScript, a class is a way of providing a structure and interface for creating and interacting with objects (for more information see Mozilla, 2020a).

Client: For front-end developers the client is usually the browser. Front-end developers work client-side.

Compiler: A program which converts one programming language into a lower-level programming language, eventually down to machine code.

Content delivery network (CDN): A CDN is a geographically distributed set of servers that host and serve identical content. Because they are spread around the world, the closest (and thus fastest) serves the resource to the client.

CSS object model (CSSOM): The CSSOM is a representation of all the CSS on a web page. It can be manipulated, in the same way as the DOM can be manipulated, by JavaScript.

Database abstraction layer (DBAL or DAL): A DBAL provides a uniform interface for programs to use when communicating with any (usually SQL-based) database.

Dependencies: JavaScript is likely the most used programming language in the world. Sometimes we will find functions and libraries which we can make use of within our own work, so we add them as dependencies. This means we don't have to reinvent the wheel if someone has already written what we need.

Dependency source tree: This lists the dependencies for a project so that we don't need to save all our dependencies when we make backups of our work. It also means we can download only our work and recreate the application later by downloading the specified versions of the listed dependencies.

Document object model (DOM): The DOM is a representation of all the HTML markup on a web page. It can be manipulated or wholly created by JavaScript.

ECMAScript: ECMAScript is the evolving standard which JavaScript conforms to.

Element: In HTML an element is a component of the document. It can have one, many or no attributes. It will have at least one parent (if it isn't the `html` element) and can have one, many or no children within it.

Engine: A browser engine converts HTML markup into a DOM. There is also a JavaScript engine, which executes the JavaScript code in the page. Search engines are used to retrieve information from diverse sources.

ES6: Otherwise known as ECMAScript 2015 or JavaScript 6, this is an updated ECMAScript specification. The latest version at the time of writing is ES2020.

Evergreen browser: Browsers which automatically update and upgrade to the latest version.

Expression: An expression is something which can be evaluated into a Boolean – a test, if you will.

Extending: In CSS, this is the process of extending a class with extra styling.

Extensible Markup Language (XML): XML is a markup language similar to HTML and with roots in SGML. It was designed to store and transport data.

Feature phone: Generally a phone with only a numerical input and limited multimedia or internet capabilities. Sometimes also known as a 'dumb phone'.

Framework: JavaScript frameworks dictate how the application should be structured.

Front-end: The part of the website with which the user interacts, made up of HTML, which can be decorated with CSS, and enhanced with JavaScript.

Graphical user interface (GUI): Pronounced 'gooey', it is the user interface with which we interact with phones and computers, with clickable icons representing programs or actions.

Handler: An event handler is a JavaScript function which is called when an event occurs.

Hello World: A 'Hello World' is a program which displays 'Hello World' and illustrates how a programming language works. The Hello World Collection (http://helloworldcollection.de) is a collection of 'Hello World' programs in many computer programming languages.

HyperText Markup Language (HTML): Tim Berners-Lee, inspired by Charles Goldfarb's SGML, developed HTML to display data on the internet.

Interpreter: An interpreter executes programs without them having been compiled into a lower-level programming language.

Java Applet: A Java Applet is a program written in Java which can be embedded within a web page.

JavaScript (JS): An interpreted programming language.

JavaScript Object Notation (JSON): A human-readable file format used for storing data made up of key–value pairs.

JavaScript tagging: A way of collecting information about what a user does on a website or application.

JavaScript XML (JSX): A way of representing HTML within JavaScript, primarily used in React.

JSFiddle: An online integrated development environment for HTML, CSS and JavaScript.

Library: A collection of functions, often all associated with one area, such as numbers or dates.

Machine code: Assembly language uses words so that humans don't need to interact with processors directly. An assembler takes assembly language and converts it to machine code (see Sims, 2016, for further explanation).

Markup: Notation added to text to give extra information about how the text should be displayed.

Meetup: An informal gathering of people to discuss a specified subject or subjects.

Minimal viable product (MVP): A version of a product which does the bare essentials required. It is used to garner data about whether an investment of effort is justified.

Model–view–controller (MVC): A design pattern with three distinct areas: the data (model), the user interface (view), and the event controllers and associated programming logic (controller).

Model–view–viewmodel (MVVM): Similar to MVC but with a slightly different architecture. Rather than having a controller, there is instead a viewmodel. The difference is discussed further in Chapter 2.

Module bundler: A program which bundles modules (see Bundler above, as they are effectively the same thing).

Module loader: Similar to module bundlers, these are JavaScript programs that retrieve and execute JavaScript modules in an order which does not cause errors.

MySQL: A relational database management system which is open source and very popular.

Native modules: Native modules remove the need for module loaders and module bundlers by providing a facility for JavaScript programs to import functionality from other JavaScript files without an external library. See Buckler (2018) for an excellent article on this topic.

Native web components: Native web components allow developers to create their own HTML elements. At present, it is only possible to do so by using a suite of different technologies.

Networking layer: The part of a browser that enables it to retrieve data from servers.

Non-functional requirement: This describes what a system should do without regard to how it does it.

NoSQL: A database which doesn't use SQL as a way of retrieving data and doesn't store its data in normalised tables.

Object-oriented programming (OOP): A way of programming which aggregates closely associated functions and values in an object.

Package manager: A program which automates the process of installing dependencies.

Parent: All elements apart from the `html` element in an HTML document have a parent.

PHP: A popular open-source server-side programming language. Created in 1994, it has evolved significantly since.

Polyfill: A plugin or piece of code that provides the technology that a browser should provide but perhaps, due to the browser not following modern standards, does not.

Post-processor: In this context, post-processors take CSS and ensure the style declarations work across multiple browsers by adding multiple prefixes for different browsers.

Pre-processor: These take styling written in one of the stylesheet languages, such as SASS, and convert it into CSS.

Pull request: A request for changed code to be merged into a codebase.

Quality assurance (QA): A means of measuring the success of the software and ensuring its quality.

React: A JavaScript framework.

Render: In this instance, the act of drawing the DOM to the browser with its associated styling from the CSSOM.

Root element: The ultimate parent of elements in an HTML document. This is the `html` element.

Scrum (Agile): A way for Agile teams to tackle problems while working to produce a finished product.

Selector: Selectors are used to find elements which need to be styled. There are many, many ways this can be accomplished but it is usually done by finding the relevant `class` or `id` attribute of an element.

Semantics: Concerned with meaning.

Server log: A record made by the server of all requests made to it.

Serverless infrastructure: Serverless infrastructure and architecture abstract the programming stack of server-side infrastructure – that is to say, the infrastructure is still there, but it is provided by a third party. Rather than paying for the provision of infrastructure, users instead pay to use the infrastructure.

Server-side infrastructure: The programming stack installed on a server. It allows the server not only to serve web pages and applications but also to store and process data.

Single-page application (SPA): In an SPA, the current page you are visiting has been entirely generated by JavaScript and navigation is mocked. Instead of the browser retrieving a new HTML document, JavaScript rewrites the current page with data retrieved from the server or the state management pattern.

Spiral: A methodology which entails a repeated process of planning, risk analysis, engineering and evaluation, designed to mitigate risks. Initially requirements are small, and during each iteration further requirements are added.

Sprint (Agile): A sprint is a period in which a feature is developed and released to a client. The duration of sprints varies, but I usually work in fortnight-long sprints.

SQL injection attack: The process whereby attackers attempt to subvert systems by placing malicious code in form inputs. Once executed, these might damage systems or lead to private data becoming public.

Standard Generalized Markup Language (SGML): An ISO standard markup language which inspired both HTML and XML. It was developed to display documents in different formats, such as on the internet or in print. Versions of HTML prior to HTML5 could still be parsed as SGML.

Stand-up (Agile): A meeting, usually held every morning, in which a team discusses progress, plans and impediments. They are called stand-ups because traditionally attendees had to remain standing and this encouraged terse reports.

State management pattern: A state management pattern allows the state of your application to be shared among all components of that application.

Story (Agile): A description of what will be achieved as a result of some work carried out in a sprint. A sprint can have many stories.

Structured Query Language (SQL): A language used to create, read, update and delete information within a relational database. There are many different types of SQL, which is why sometimes a database abstraction layer is used.

Style sheet: An external file containing CSS referenced within the head of an HTML document. The file is downloaded by the browser and used as part of the process of generating the CSSOM.

Toolchain: A set of other programs used in development. For instance, CSS and JavaScript toolchains generate CSS and JavaScript for consumption by browsers, perhaps from languages other than CSS or JavaScript.

Transpilation: The process of converting one programming language into another. Most often in front-end development we talk of transpiling TypeScript into JavaScript.

Use case: In most instances, front-end developers use the term 'use case' as a substitute for 'situation'. Different situations or use cases require different approaches.

User: The user of the application we are developing and the focus of the front-end developer.

User eXperience (UX): The experience of a user while interacting with the web page or application.

User interface (UI): The front-end of a web page or application.

Version control system: A way of ensuring changes to a codebase are tracked and can be reversed.

Viewport: The browser window. This is most often in portrait orientation on mobile devices and landscape on desktops or laptops.

Vue: A JavaScript framework.

Waterfall: A methodology which emphasises a logical approach to development. It has been criticised for being rigid and ignoring feedback during the development process.

Web template engine: Most often a server-side technology. It abstracts the generation of HTML and can mean that repetitive blocks of code can be stored in a separate file and inserted by the server-side application when pages are requested by the browser.

What you see is what you get (WYSIWYG): An editor in which the final product closely resembles that which the editor sees while editing.

INDEX